TURN ME ON,
DEAD MAN

❖ REFERENCE SERIES ❖

1 ALL TOGETHER NOW
The First Complete Beatles
Discography, 1961-1975
by Harry Castleman & Walter J. Podrazik

2 THE BEATLES AGAIN
[Sequel to All Together Now]
by Harry Castleman & Walter J. Podrazik

3 A DAY IN THE LIFE
The Beatles Day-By-Day, 1960-1970
by Tom Schultheiss

4 THINGS WE SAID TODAY
The Complete Lyrics and a Concordance
to The Beatles Songs, 1962-1970
by Colin Campbell & Allan Murphy

5 YOU CAN'T DO THAT
Beatles Bootlegs
& Novelty Records, 1963-1980
by Charles Reinhart

6 SURF'S UP!
The Beach Boys On Record, 1961-1981
by Brad Elliott

7 COLLECTING THE BEATLES
An Introduction & Price Guide to Fab Four
Collectibles, Records & Memorabilia
by Barbara Fenick

8 JAILHOUSE ROCK
The Bootleg Records of
Elvis Presley, 1970-1983
by Lee Cotten & Howard DeWitt

9 THE LITERARY LENNON:
A COMEDY OF LETTERS
The First Study of All the Major and Minor
Writings of John Lennon
by Dr. James Sauceda

10 THE END OF THE BEATLES?
[Sequel to The Beatles Again and
All Together Now]
by Harry Castleman & Walter J. Podrazik

11 HERE, THERE & EVERYWHERE
The First International Beatles
Bibliography, 1962-1982
by Carol D. Terry

12 CHUCK BERRY--ROCK 'N' ROLL MUSIC
Second Edition, Revised
by Howard A. DeWitt

13 ALL SHOOK UP
Elvis Day-By-Day, 1954-1977
by Lee Cotten

14 WHO'S NEW WAVE IN MUSIC
An Illustrated Encyclopedia, 1976-1982
by David Bianco

15 THE ILLUSTRATED DISCOGRAPHY
OF SURF MUSIC, 1961-1965
Second Edition, Revised
by John Blair

16 COLLECTING THE BEATLES, VOLUME 2
An Introduction & Price Guide to Fab Four
Collectibles, Records & Memorabilia
by Barbara Fenick

17 HEART OF STONE
The Definitive Rolling Stones
Discography, 1962-1983
by Felix Aeppli

18 BEATLEFAN
The Authoritative Publication of Record
For Fans of the Beatles, Volumes 1 & 2
Reprint Edition, With Additions

19 YESTERDAY'S PAPERS
The Rolling Stones In Print, 1963-1984
by Jessica MacPhail

20 EVERY LITTLE THING
The Definitive Guide To Beatles
Recording Variations, Rare Mixes &
Other Musical Oddities, 1958-1986
by William McCoy & Mitchell McGeary

21 STRANGE DAYS
The Music Of John, Paul, George & Ringo
Twenty Years On
by Walter J. Podrazik

22 SEQUINS & SHADES
The Michael Jackson Reference Guide
by Carol D. Terry

23 WILD & INNOCENT
The Recordings of
Bruce Springsteen, 1973-1985
by Brad Elliott

24 TIME IS ON MY SIDE
The Rolling Stones
Day-By-Day, 1962-1986
by Alan Stewart & Cathy Sanford

25 HEATWAVE
The Motown Fact Book
by David Bianco

26 BEATLEFAN
The Authoritative Publication of Record
For Fans of the Beatles, Volumes 3 & 4
Reprint Edition, With Additions

27 RECONSIDER BABY
The Definitive Elvis
Sessionography, 1954-1977
by Ernst Jorgensen, Erik Rasmussen &
Johnny Mikkelsen

28 THE MONKEES:
A MANUFACTURED IMAGE
The Ultimate Reference Guide to
Monkee Memories & Memorabilia
by Ed Reilly, Maggie McManus &
Bill Chadwick

29 RETURN TO SENDER
The First Complete Discography Of Elvis
Tribute & Novelty Records, 1956-1986
by Howard Banney

30 THE CHILDREN OF NUGGETS
The Definitive Guide To
"Psychedelic Sixties" Punk Rock
On Compilation Albums
by David Walters

31 SHAKE, RATTLE & ROLL
The Golden Age Of American Rock 'N' Roll,
Volume 1: 1952-1955
by Lee Cotten

Available only through Popular Culture, Ink., P.O. Box 1839, Ann Arbor, Michigan 48106
Phone: 1-800-678-8828

32 THE ILLUSTRATED DISCOGRAPHY
OF HOT ROD MUSIC, 1961-1965
by John Blair & Stephen McParland

33 POSITIVELY BOB DYLAN
A Thirty-Year Discography, Concert &
Recording Session Guide, 1960-1991
by Michael Krogsgaard

34 OFF THE RECORD
Motown By Master Number, 1959-1989
Volume 1: Singles
by Reginald J. Bartlette

35 LISTENING TO THE BEATLES
An Audiophile's Guide to the
Sound of the Fab Four, Volume 1: Singles
by David Schwartz

36 ELVIS—THE SUN YEARS
The Story Of Elvis Presley In The Fifties
by Howard A. DeWitt

37 HEADBANGERS
The Worldwide MegaBook Of
Heavy Metal Bands
by Mark Hale

38 THAT'S ALL
Bobby Darin On Record,
Stage & Screen
by Jeff Bleiel

❖ REMEMBRANCES SERIES ❖

1 AS I WRITE THIS LETTER
An American Generation
Remembers The Beatles
Edited by Marc A. Catone

2 THE LONGEST COCKTAIL PARTY
An Insider's Diary of The Beatles,
Their Million-Dollar Apple Empire
and Its Wild Rise and Fall
Reprint Edition, With Additions
by Richard DiLello

3 AS TIME GOES BY
Living In The Sixties
Reprint Edition, With Additions
by Derek Taylor

4 A CELLARFUL OF NOISE
Reprint Edition, With Additions
by Brian Epstein

5 THE BEATLES AT THE BEEB
The Story Of Their Radio Career, 1962-1965
Reprint Edition, With Additions
by Kevin Howlett

6 THE BEATLES READER
A Selection Of Contemporary Views, News,
& Reviews Of The Beatles In Their Heyday
Edited by Charles P. Neises

7 THE BEATLES DOWN UNDER
The 1964 Australia & New Zealand Tour
Reprint Edition, With Additions
by Glenn A. Baker

8 LONG LONELY HIGHWAY
A 1950's Elvis Scrapbook
Reprint Edition, With Additions
by Ger Rijff

9 IKE'S BOYS
The Story Of The Everly Brothers
by Phyllis Karpp

10 ELVIS—FROM MEMPHIS TO HOLLYWOOD
Memories From My Twelve Years
With Elvis Presley
by Alan Fortas

11 SAVE THE LAST DANCE FOR ME
The Musical Legacy Of The Drifters,
1953-1993
by Tony Allan with Faye Treadwell

12 TURN ME ON, DEAD MAN
The Complete Story of the
Paul McCartney Death Hoax
by Andru J. Reeve

❖ TRIVIA SERIES ❖

1 NOTHING IS BEATLEPROOF
Advanced Beatles Trivia
For Fab Four Fanciers
by Mike Hockinson

Available only through Popular Culture, Ink., P.O. Box 1839, Ann Arbor, Michigan 48106
Phone: 1-800-678-8828

PAUL McCartney in concert, 1990
Paul plays a few songs for his New York audience.
(Photo courtesy Bill Last/Liverpool Productions.)

TURN ME ON, DEAD MAN

The Complete Story of the Paul McCartney Death Hoax

by
Andru J. Reeve

Popular Culture, Ink.
1994

Book design and layout by Tom Schultheiss.
Cover design by Patricia Curtis and Tom Schultheiss..
Computer programming by Alex Przebienda.

All cover art is copyright © 1994,
by Popular Culture, Ink.
All Rights Reserved.

ISBN 1-56075-035-9
LC 93-86666

Published by Popular Culture, Ink.
P.O. Box 1839, Ann Arbor, MI 48106 USA

PCI Collector Editions
are published especially for discerning collectors and libraries.
Each Collector Edition title is released in limited quantities
identified by edition, printing number, and number of copies.
Unlike trade editions, they are not generally available in bookstores.

10 9 8 7 6 5 4 3 2 1
(First edition, first printing: 1000 copies)

Printed in the United States of America

"The best rock-and-roll books in the world!"

Contents

INTRODUCTION .... **xi**

ACKNOWLEDGEMENTS .... **xiv**

Part I: The Story

CHAPTER 1: Paul Is A Dead Man **1**

CHAPTER 2: You Were In A Car Crash **7**

CHAPTER 3: Bang! Bang! Maxwell's Silver Hammer **9**

CHAPTER 4: So Long, Paul **13**

CHAPTER 5: I Read The News Today, Oh Boy **17**

CHAPTER 6: Nothing To Do To Save His Life **25**

CHAPTER 7: O, Untimely Death **31**

CHAPTER 8: He Blew His Mind Out In A Car **33**

CHAPTER 9: We Don't Often Sing Or Refer To Death **39**

CHAPTER 10: There's So Much Evidence That It
Couldn't Be A Coincidence **45**

CHAPTER 11: Paul Died In An Earthquake In Mexico
In 1967 .... **51**

CHAPTER 12: I Was Alone, I Took A Ride **55**

CHAPTER 13: I Heard The Radio The Other Day **59**

CHAPTER 14: When You Were Stoned, You Could
Always Find Clues.................................... **65**

CHAPTER 15: One And One And One Is Three **73**

CHAPTER 16: I Know What It's Like To Be Dead................. **81**

CHAPTER 17: With Lovers And Friends, I Still Can Recall . **91**

CHAPTER 18: Open Up Your Eyes Now................................. **99**

CHAPTER 19: Hey, It's Just Insanity.................................... **103**

CHAPTER 20: Don't Be Surprised If You Hear Rumors
That I'm Dead.. **107**

CHAPTER 21: America! America! You Want To Believe
In Miracles **111**

ix

CHAPTER 22: We Get Letters From All Sorts Of Nuts **119**
CHAPTER 23: Do I Look Dead? I'm As Fit As A Fiddle **123**
CHAPTER 24: I Managed To Stay Alive Through It All **129**
CHAPTER 25: America Is Such A Fanatical Place **139**

EPILOGUE: **147**
ADDENDUM: Ringo, Paul, George And John **149**

Part II: Appendices

APPENDIX   I: Here's Another Clue For You All **153**
APPENDIX II: "The Curious Case Of The 'Death' Of
                     Paul McCartney," by Barbara Suczek **173**
APPENDIX III: Other Significant Rumors About
                     The Beatles **191**

AFTERWORD, by Joel Glazier: **197**

ADDITIONAL READING: **201**

INDEX: **211**

Introduction

In October of 1969, Paul McCartney of the Beatles was dead.

Or so thought hundreds of thousands of young people—first in the Midwestern United States, then throughout the country and, finally, around the globe. But it wasn't true. McCartney, in his own words, was "alive and living in Scotland."

The "Paul-is-Dead" rumor was far from ordinary gossip. The fascinating aspect of this rumor was that it involved an elaborate theory. It was proposed that McCartney had died from injuries sustained in a fiery car crash during the winter of 1966. The surviving Beatles, unwilling to risk their popularity, kept the death a secret and replaced Paul with the winner of a look-a-like contest held in Great Britain. The Beatles then let the public know about the ruse by planting dozens of "clues" on their album covers and in their music. These clues ran the gamut from Paul's bare feet on the cover of **Abbey Road** to alleged backwards messages such as "turn me on, dead man" in the song "Revolution 9."

Although there were antecedents, the first large-scale public awareness of the story occurred on October 12, 1969 in Detroit, Michigan. WKNR-FM disc jockey Russ Gibb received a phone call from a young man named Tom who told him that if he played a Beatles album backwards, he would hear a suggestion of Paul's death. Gibb did as instructed and he was soon swamped with calls from the radio audience. In the days to follow, more clues were discovered and the rumor took off from there.

No other rumor, before or since, has sparked a public

response as intense, complex, and unyielding as the "Paul-is-Dead" controversy. All three network news programs, the top newspapers and thousands of radio stations gave the story coverage. College campuses became clue centers, with students abandoning their regular studies in order to devote time toward the unearthing of more secret messages in the grooves of four Beatles albums: **Sgt. Pepper's Lonely Hearts Club Band, Magical Mystery Tour, The Beatles** (aka, "White Album") and **Abbey Road**. The late disc jockey Bob Lewis, of WPLJ in New York, dubbed these student sleuths "cluesters." Two of the most well-versed cluesters, Fred LaBour (University of Michigan) and John Summer (Ohio Wesleyan University) became local celebrities and were sought-after for media interviews from every corner of the world.

In the beginning, Paul McCartney refused to dignify the rumor with a response to the media. His silence only served to add fuel to a raging inferno of innuendo and he was soon forced out of hiding to denounce his demise via telephone. One day later, he was photographed with his family en route to his private Scottish retreat. *Life* magazine followed McCartney to his farmhouse hideaway and made the rumor the cover story of its November 7 issue. It became irrefutable: Paul McCartney was alive and kicking.

However, this did not completely quell the rumor. Instead, it took on a different level. The secret messages *were still there*, said the cluesters. It was then surmised that the Beatles and/or their record label had concocted a death hoax in order to sell more albums. Both parties flatly denied the allegation, but there was no denying that sales did indeed skyrocket during the last months of 1969. In fact, Rocco Catena, vice-president of marketing for Capitol Records, proudly boasted that "this is going to be our biggest month in terms of Beatles sales" when queried about the rumor.

Near the end of November, the rumor died as quickly as it had been born. Perhaps there were no more clues to be found. Or maybe Paul's denials began to have the desired effect. To this day, over twenty years later, many questions still remain unanswered and a great part of the story has never been told.

How did the rumor start? Who started it? Why did it spread with such an intensity? Did the Beatles play a giant cosmic joke on their fans?

This book presents the most complete and accurate account of what transpired during an unforgettable four-week period in the fall of 1969.* It's the story about the effects of an unrelenting rumor, but it's also the story about the people who found themselves immersed in something that seemed to take on a life of its own.

Shall we dig in?

---

*If you need to refresh your memory on what caused all of the excitement, Appendix I offers a compendium of seventy "clues" that were discovered on Beatles record albums.

Acknowledgements

To thank everyone who has helped in some way on this project would fill several pages. But...let's give it the old college try.

First and foremost, a gracious thank you has to go to Russ Gibb, Fred LaBour and John Summer, whose stories form the skeleton of this book. Thank you all for allowing me into your memories and experiences. A special thanks to all three of you for sharing printed material with me, particularly Fred LaBour for the gracious permission to reprint your vital article from the *Michigan Daily*, Russ Gibb for permission to transcribe segments of your WKNR radio shows, and John Summer for supplying rare UPI wire scripts and newspaper articles.

Thank you to Christopher Glenn of CBS radio for sharing your memories of the meeting with Paul's brother on Mike Douglas' TV show. Thanks to Richard Pecard for telling me the story of Mr. Pony-Tail in Dupont Circle Park. And, to Colby Andersson, my appreciation goes for the eerie episode about the secret on the cover of *Life* magazine.

No less appreciated are the efforts of Peter Mooney from the University of Michigan who dug up archival material for me, including the October 14 issue of the *Michigan Daily*. Closer to home, thanks to all the great folks at the Library of Congress in Washington, D.C. So many of you lent a hand in my search for the hundreds of newspaper and magazine articles I needed.

Thank you to Suzanne Lewis from the EMI Music Archives, who helped me track down the identity of Lord Sitar and also provided vital information about record release dates. And a similar nod of gratitude to the many good people at Capitol Records. I hope you will forgive me for some of my comments about the "butcher" era; I sincerely believe those days are long in the past. You were all a great help to me!

Thank you to all of the Universities who allowed me access to their alumni lists. And, while we're in the neighborhood, thanks to Heather Reed for sending me the Tim Harper article that appeared in the Drake University *Times-Delphic*.

And the same to Jerry Thompson of Northern Illinois University for the *Northern Star* clipping.

How could I forget David Hicks, president of Hicks Broadcasting, for steering me in the direction of Russ Gibb? Thank you, David.

A special thanks to the Vanderbilt TV News Archives for having the foresight to record and save network newscasts (the networks didn't begin the practice of preserving their own airchecks until 1975!).

Thank you to John Mainelli of WABC Radio for attempting to locate Roby Yonge. Where are you, Roby?

Thank you, Frank Davies, for talking to me about your career with Klaatu. My apologies to you and the band for not following my original plan and making the Klaatu Rumor a larger part of my project. Your time and effort, however, is greatly appreciated and I wish you all well. And please see to it that the remaining Klaatu albums get reissued on compact disc!

To all of the readers of *Goldmine* magazine ("The Bible of Record Collectors") who responded to my ads, THANK YOU! Without the vintage radio programs and other items supplied by Jonathan White, Robert "Parks" Parker, John Bulette, John Fox, Duane Zehring, Rodney Morgan, Randy Hall in Ontario, Jerry Kunny and Paul Walser, there would have been little flesh on the skeleton.

I haven't forgotten Dartanyan Brown or Tim Harper. Thank you both for the reminiscences. And thank you to David Lock, Michael LaBricque, Jonathan Newberry, Bob "Beatle Boy" Becker, Pat Corcoran, Marilyn Denbloch, Rick Sandherst, and Steve Smith for your time and comments. To those of you who didn't want your names used, thanks to each and everyone of you...you know who you are.

Thank you, Joel Buckner of Conroe, Texas (the best Beatles memorabilia dealer in the world), for finding and sending me an audio tape of the F. Lee Bailey "Paul-is-Dead" television show. Now, who out there has a *videotape* of the show?

Thanks to Howard K. Smith (former ABC anchor) and

John Chancellor (NBC correspondent) for chatting with me about the rumor.

A special bow of gratitude to John Sayers and my sister Vicki Reeve for spending hours of your time scanning and processing this manuscript and helping me grow acclimated to that beast known as the Word Processor. You guys saved me hours of time in the preparation of the final draft, and I really do appreciate it!

Thank you to Victor Keegan for granting permission to reprint your article from *The Guardian* and for sharing your memories with me.

Thank you to Barbara Suczek for your permission to reprint your brilliant sociological study of the rumor, "The Curious Case of the 'Death' of Paul McCartney" which first appeared in 1972 in the premiere issue of *Urban Life and Culture*.

And a tip of the hat to all the authors out there who have attempted to write this story. Many have tried, and I know now why it took this long to get onto paper!

And most important of all, thank you John, Paul, George and Ringo. You made my life a little more valuable with your music.

One final thank you...to whomever started the "Paul-is-Dead" rumor. Without you, all of this would have been unimaginable, even to the best fiction writer.

I.
"Paul Is A Dead Man...
Miss Him, Miss Him, Miss Him...."
—A clue found at the end of the song "I'm So Tired"

"This is WKNR-FM...Uncle Russ here. Let's go to the phone lines..." As he did every Sunday during his shift, disc jockey Russ Gibb was working the telephones. Being the fledgling medium that it was in 1969, FM radio was extremely open to the suggestions of its small but dedicated audience. Correctly labeled "underground radio" by the trade journals, stations like WKNR in Detroit, Michigan, broadcasted a progressive rock format with a playlist that would change on a daily basis. Beyond receiving requests for songs, deejays like Gibb simply wanted to "rap" with their listeners; to exchange ideologies over the airwaves. Uncle Russ, as he was known to his audience, had just finished playing a few songs from the new Beatles album **Abbey Road** when he decided to go to the phone lines.

"Who do we have here? What's your name?"

The reply came from a young voice filtered through phone static. "Uh, this is Tom on the line."

"Yeah, hello Tom. What's going down?"

Tom began to respond, but Gibb interrupted. "Have you got your radio on?"

"Yeah, a little bit..."

"Well, turn it down, man," Gibb admonished, "'cause you're giving us feedback."

Tom did as instructed and returned to the phone. "I was going to rap with you about McCartney being dead and what is this all about?"

Unseen by his audience, Gibb rolled his eyes skyward. Not another one of these superstar death rumors! Remembering the similar story that he had heard about Bob Dylan only a couple of years back, the disbelieving deejay decided to educate the kid.

"First, what school do you go to?"

"I go to Eastern Michigan University."

"You go to Eastern Michigan University and you heard

1

Russ Gibb (circa 1969)
"Uncle Russ" picked up the telephone while on the air at WKNR-FM Detroit.
The October 12 call from "Tom" led to the discovery of several clues
that pointed to the death of Paul McCartney.
(Photo courtesy Russ Gibb.)

that McCartney is dead?"

"Yeah, that's right."

Uncle Russ then began to recount some of the stories he had heard concerning either the well-being or sexual preference of various rock 'n' roll musicians. "Look," Gibb concluded, "that story is always floating around about somebody, but it's just not true."

The caller was undaunted by Gibb's skepticism. "There are clues to McCartney's death in the records. What you've got to do is play 'Revolution Number Nine' backwards."

Gibb suddenly became interested. Play a record backwards? It was a line of thinking that Russ Gibb found instantly appealing, perhaps because only a short time earlier, the deejay had been calling himself "Bbig Ssur" on the air. Gibb used to tell his listeners on ongoing fable in which he was one of the Starpeople who came to earth in a spaceship. The craft landed in Big Sur, California. His mission on the planet would be detected if he didn't have an earth name, so he simply took the name from a sign he saw reversed in the spaceship's rear-view mirror. 'WELCOME TO BIG SUR' became 'RUS GIB OT EMOCLEW', but he decided to shorten it to RUS(S) GIB(B). Little mind games like this were always a part of the Detroit deejay's act.

"So, did you hear about playing 'Revolution Number Nine' backwards?" Tom repeated.

Gibb shifted his posture in his chair, edging closer to the microphone. "No, I haven't heard about that."

"Well, what you have to do is play 'Number Nine' backwards and it's supposed to reveal a secret message."

The Beatles' "White Album" had already found its way into Gibb's hand before the youth had finished his statement. Continuing his on-the-air conversation, he placed side four of the record on one of the empty turntables and moved the needle over the selection entitled "Revolution 9." This was one of the Beatles' oddest works to date. A montage of random sound effects and voices rather than a true song, "Revolution 9" was a product of John Lennon's relationship with avant-garde artist Yoko Ono. It contained scant participation from the other Beatles.

"Now what part am I supposed to play?" Gibb asked as he

switched off the turntable's motor.

"Play the part where the voice keeps saying, 'number nine...number nine'."

Placing the needle on the appropriate groove, Gibb opened up the audio fader so that Tom and the rest of the audience could hear the results. With a steady hand and constant speed, he then turned the disc counter-clockwise and listened.

The voice which had been repeating the phrase "number nine" when going in the forward direction was now intoning something quite different. Clearly, the voice was chanting "turn me on, dead man...turn me on, dead man..."

"Wow," thought Gibb to himself, "oh man, that's weird."

Gibb's concentration was abruptly broken by the woosh of the studio door as it flew open. Turning around, he saw the beet-red face of the staff engineer.

"What the hell are you doing to my goddamn equipment," he roared more than inquired, "you're gonna ruin the machine!"

Brushing aside his shoulder-length brown hair, Uncle Russ attempted to calm the engineer. "Look, I've stumbled onto something. Hang tight and I'll fill you in."

"Goddamn hippie crap," the engineer grunted under his breath. He turned to leave Gibb with his caller.

"See, it says 'turn me on, dead man,'" Tom piped, "and there are a lot more clues..."

Dan Carlisle, the disc jockey whose show followed Gibb's, was pulling records from the station's library and listening to the odd phone conversation. He stopped what he was doing and hustled into the broadcast booth.

"Russ," Carlisle said, "what's going on?"

Placing a finger to his lips to indicate that he was still on the air, Gibb continued to speak to Tom from EMU. Before he could find out about some of the other clues, he noticed a freckle-faced young man entering the studio. He carried with him a copy of the Beatles' **Magical Mystery Tour** album. Gibb told the audience to stay tuned, and went to a commercial as the uninvited guest approached the deejay.

"Hey, I live down the street and I heard your phone call," explained the youth, "but I'll show you a clue that *really* proves

4

McCartney is dead." He pulled the vinyl disc from its jacket and passed it to Gibb. "Play the very end of 'Strawberry Fields Forever'."

"Well, man, what does it say?"

"Play it and you'll hear Lennon say, 'I buried Paul'." Gibb turned to his microphone. "You're tuned to WKNR-FM," he informed his listeners, "and we have someone in the studio who agrees with Tom. He's asked me to play another song that contains a clue that points to the possibility of Paul McCartney's death."

The deejay and his audience listened together for the eerie passage on "Strawberry Fields Forever."

Twenty miles from the studios of WKNR, on the road that led out of Ann Arbor, University of Michigan sophomore Fred LaBour was driving to nearby Jackson to visit with his relatives. Feeling miserable after an argument with his girlfriend, LaBour switched on the car radio so he could lose himself in the music.

When he flipped the dial to WKNR, he lost himself in something else.

Fᴿᴇᴅ LᴀBᴏᴜʀ (ᴄɪʀᴄᴀ 1969)
University of Michigan sophomore Fred LaBour heard Russ Gibb's
mysterious radio show and responded with an unusual record review of the
Beatles' **Abbey Road** album in the student newspaper, the *Michigan Daily*.
(Photo courtesy Fred LaBour.)

II.
"You Were In A Car Crash
And You Lost Your Hair"
—"Don't Pass Me By"
by the Beatles

The University of Michigan originally occupied 3,840 acres of land that had been donated by the local Indian tribes. In 1837, the University was moved to its present location in Ann Arbor and a total of nine students were enrolled. By the mid-1900s, it was only one of a cluster of colleges that had sprung up in the Detroit area.

As with scores of other campuses across the United States in 1969, studies at the University of Michigan took a back seat to "consciousness raising." Students were more concerned with the unpopular war in Vietnam than they were with the dusty history of the Constitution. History was something that could not be changed; however, the conflict in Asia and the U.S. government's decision to be involved in it was a situation that could be dealt with *now*. Young people truly believed that they could make a difference through their actions, and anti-war protests were a daily fixture in their lives.

Fred LaBour, while as concerned as any of his fellow students, was more engrossed in the pursuit of his interests in music and writing. In fact, he often combined his interests and wrote record reviews for the University's student paper, *The Michigan Daily*. This week there was a slot open for his review of the new Beatles album **Abbey Road**, and LaBour had been pondering an angle which would be more original than simply writing about the merit of the songs and the production. He was looking for something a little bit different......

The bubbles of static on LaBour's car radio ceased as he found his favorite station just to the right of "100" on the Sparkomatic's glass face. The first thing he heard was Uncle Russ speaking in the low, pause-filled manner that had become his trademark.

"So...we just got this phone call from this guy Tom who says McCartney is dead. And we found...and heard...some clues

7

to his death. But, look, here's a clue you can't hear. Get your copy of the **Magical Mystery Tour** album and turn to the last page in the souvenir booklet..."

LaBour cocked his head toward the radio as a quizzical eyebrow rose above his wire-rimmed glasses. "McCartney dead?" he wondered aloud. "What is this?"

Later that evening, LaBour returned to campus just in time to begin his job as a ticket-taker at the Cinema Guild. His friend Jay Cassidy was already tearing ticket stubs at the entrance when he ambled up to the theatre.

"Hey, Jay," Fred said as he slapped his friend on the back, "how's it goin'?"

"Fine, swine," joked Cassidy as he handed a fistful of torn blue stubs to LaBour. "Now get to work."

"Jay, did you hear Russ Gibb's show this afternoon?"

"No. Why? Did he say 'shit' on the air or something?"

Fred grinned but he didn't laugh. "No, it wasn't anything like that. Uncle Russ got this phone call from a guy at EMU who claimed that Paul McCartney was dead and—"

"I didn't hear about that," interrupted Cassidy. "That's gotta be bull."

"Wait, there's more. The guy on the phone said that the Beatles have been putting messages on their records that hint that Paul is dead!"

Cassidy listened to LaBour's description of the radio show between their ticket tearing and was soon able to sum up the entire event.

"The guy's nuts," offered Jay, "but wouldn't it be wild if there was this whole plot? You know, like a conspiracy to hide the truth from the public, but sort of let it leak out so that eventually someone would get wise to it?"

Walking home from his job that night, Fred LaBour knew that he finally had an angle for his record review.

8

III.

**"Bang! Bang! Maxwell's Silver Hammer
Came Down Upon His Head
Bang! Bang! Maxwell's Silver Hammer
Made Sure That He Was Dead"**
—"Maxwell's Silver Hammer"
by the Beatles

In 1968, the Beatles were firmly established as the re-cording industry's trend-setters. By giving up touring in 1966, they were able to devote more time and energy to the creative process, thus enabling them to come up with complex recordings like **Sgt. Pepper's Lonely Hearts Club Band** and **Magical Mystery Tour.** Each new recording that was issued virtually instituted a new standard for other musical artists to aspire.

In May of 1968, the Beatles set a precedent of a different sort. John and Paul flew to America and announced to the press that the group was inaugurating its own entertainment empire, to be called Apple. It would include a record label (to be distrib-uted by Capitol in the U.S. and EMI for "The Rest of the World"), a studio, a film division, and a music publishing coop-erative. Paul dubbed this an experiment in "Western Commu-nism" and sent an open invitation to all would-be writers, musicians and filmmakers. "We want to set up a system whereby people...don't have to go on their knees in somebody's office— probably yours," Lennon quipped to the assemblage of record executives present at the press conference.

Acts began to be signed up at an alarming rate. James Taylor, Badfinger, Mary Hopkin, Jackie Lomax, Billy Preston, Hot Chocolate, and the Modern Jazz Quartet all became mem-bers of the Apple family. Almost immediately, Badfinger was on top of the charts with the McCartney-penned "Come And Get It." Hopkin, Preston and Hot Chocolate also made strong show-ings with their debut Apple singles. At the outset, the decision to initiate a Beatles-controlled entertainment empire seemed to be a stroke of genius.

The Beatles' own recording output during this period was staggering. "Hey Jude," their first single on the Apple label,

PAUL McCARTNEY (WINTER 1968)
Looking very much alive, Paul arrives at his home in St. John's Wood,
London, in the winter of 1968.
(Photo from the author's collection.)

became the longest song (at 7:11) to reach the top of the pop singles chart. This was followed in November by a double-album simply titled **The Beatles** (although its stark white cover inspired record-buyers and critics to dub it the "White Album"). Although devoid of the unusual instrumentation of the previous two albums, the double set was actually more "psychedelic" than it appeared at first glance. Nearly every style of contemporary popular music—blues, country & western, heavy metal, vaudeville, soul and baroque—was represented. The lyrics, too, reached a new high. "Happiness Is A Warm Gun," "Dear Prudence," and "I'm So Tired" displayed an emerging maturity and awareness that wasn't evident on previous efforts. Adding to the atmosphere was the inclusion of extraneous studio chatter in between many of the songs. The whistling, cheering and laughter seemed to indicate that the group was once again guaranteeing a splendid time to be had by all.

But tensions were rife during the recording of the "White Album." Ringo Starr quit the band, only to return a week later. John Lennon brought his new love, Yoko Ono, to many of the sessions—a development that the other Beatles found annoying. And, despite the title of the work, **The Beatles** proved to be the least group-oriented effort yet. "It was just me and a backing group, Paul and a backing group..." Lennon later stated in an interview. Indeed, Lennon and McCartney took full advantage of the new eight-track recording technology and often overdubbed all of the instruments themselves. Aside from "Birthday," none of the songs credited to "Lennon/McCartney" were true collaborations; John wrote his songs and Paul took complete charge of his creations. The "White Album" wasn't really a Beatles recording at all; it was a four-way solo album.

Meanwhile, the Apple headquarters at 3 Savile Row was experiencing financial difficulty after only a few months of operation. The people hired to run the company were taking full advantage of the situation, often purchasing immense quantities of liquor and drugs for the daily in-house parties. Company cars and office equipment began to disappear. Money was being siphoned out of the Apple coffers for improbable projects and

11

unrealized visions. "Apple is losing money," Lennon told *Disc* magazine in January of 1969. "If it carries on like this, we'll be broke in six months."

Allen Klein, a New York attorney with a long history in the music business, got wind of Lennon's remark and jetted to London to convince the Beatles that he was the answer to their problems. John, George and Ringo were impressed with Klein's credentials and reputation, and wanted to sign him up as their new business manager. Only Paul McCartney stood in the way of this arrangement.

Back in 1968 in New York, Paul had met and fallen in love with Linda Eastman, a professional rock 'n' roll photographer. By March 12, 1969, the final bachelor in the Beatles had tied the knot. Linda's father, Lee Eastman, happened to be a corporate attorney and Paul decided that the Beatles should sign him on as their new manager. The other Beatles would have nothing to do with this; they were adamant in their choice of Klein. This rift between Paul McCartney and the rest of the band would prove to be the biggest nail in the Beatles' coffin.

Nevertheless, the group forged on. After a disastrous attempt to "Get Back" to their roots with the "Let It Be" sessions, Paul convinced the rest of the band and producer George Martin to begin work on an album that would be issued in October 1969 as **Abbey Road**. Unlike the "White Album," the Beatles played together on nearly every track of this new project. Throughout the spring and summer of 1969, Paul would stroll over to the recording studio from his home around the corner where Linda was caring for their newborn daughter, Mary.

On one exceptionally-warm day in August, Paul showed up at the studio wearing sandals. During a photo session for the album cover later in the day, he took them off.

IV.
"So Long, Paul...
We Hate To See You Go"
—"So Long, Paul" by Jose Feliciano
(recording as Werbley Finster)

"Good Morning, Detroit.

"It's 7:15 on a mild Monday morning and it's time to look at the headlines on WJR...Although the bloody Sharon Tate murders remain unsolved, L.A. police said yesterday that they have a new lead provided by none other than famed crime psychic Peter Hurkos. Hurkos claimed that after handling a knife found at the scene of the crime, he saw in his mind a bearded man with a name he could only identify as 'Charlie.' Later today, Hurkos hopes to be able to lead police to a site that may hold more evidence...Also in the news, television personality Art Linkletter said Sunday that the recent suicide of his daughter was due to 'the decaying morals of the country' and he vowed to do everything possible to eradicate the drug scourge...Miss Linkletter died October 5 after leaping from the sixth floor of a Hollywood apartment complex. She was allegedly under the influence of the drug LSD...On the issue of Vietnam, President Nixon spoke in a nationally-broadcasted radio address—"

Fred LaBour slapped the side of his clock radio, ending the flow of information. He rose from bed and grabbed a pair of blue jeans that hung unceremoniously from the back of his desk chair. Slipping them on, LaBour strode over to his stereo system to begin his day with a healthy dose of rock 'n' roll. But before he could take more than a few steps, the WKNR broadcast began to replay in his head.

So...we just got this phone call from this guy named Tom who says McCartney is dead. And we found...and heard some clues to his death...

"Clues to McCartney's death," LaBour recited to himself. He knelt before the stack of record albums that rested between

13

the wood-grain speakers and quickly flipped through them.

> So far, we've found clues on **Magical Mystery Tour**...quite
> a few, actually...and one that just blows my mind, man..."I
> buried Paul"...Now, what could all this mean? Keep those
> calls coming to WKNR-FM...

LaBour chose six albums from the pile and neatly lined
them up on his desk. Taking a step back with hands on hips, he
admired the arrangement. "Yeah," he nodded, "it's all gonna fit
together."

John, Paul, George and Ringo stared back at the college
student, but their expressions didn't change. That is, except for
Paul's. He suddenly seemed to be grinning like a skeleton.

* * * * * * * * * *

The telephone intercom in Derek Taylor's office spoke a
pleasant feminine British. "Derek, the gentleman from the
States is on the line again."

The smartly-attired Beatles publicist shook his head in
amazement. Since yesterday, some disc jockey had been trying
to speak to him in reference to the well-being of Paul McCartney.
Aware that his charge had requested some privacy so that he
could spend time with his new bride Linda, Taylor had refused
to take the calls and instead issued an official statement that
all of the Beatles were on holiday. However, this time he decided
to talk to the pest.

"This is Derek Taylor."

"Hello, Derek," said the caller. It sounded as if the entire
Atlantic Ocean had joined him on the phone. "This is Russ Gibb
from WKNR in Detroit, Michigan. We're hearing all kinds of
stories over here about Paul McCartney. Is he okay?"

Taylor immediately felt a sense of deja vu. Almost three
years earlier, a rumor had swept London that McCartney had
died in a car crash during a particularly heavy January ice
storm. The rumor never took hold and it was quietly forgotten.
Could this be a revival of that old story?

"Paul McCartney is not dead, if that's what you're getting

14

at."

"Well," said Gibb, "can I speak to him then?"

"No, you cannot," replied Taylor curtly but kindly. "He's not here right now. He's on holiday with his family."

Gibb wasn't about to give up. "Derek, I really need to talk with him. The kids here are convinced that he's dead. They've found proof."

"Now—Mr. Gibbs, is it?"

"Gibb. No 's'."

"Mr. Gibb, I can assure you that Paul is fine. Don't let a few kids try and convince you otherwise."

"Okay, Derek," Gibb warned, "but I doubt this is the last time you're going to hear from me."

As Taylor placed the receiver back in its cradle, he muttered to himself, "I, too, doubt that this is the last time."

* * * * * * * * * *

When Fred LaBour walked into his afternoon English class, he saw John Gray, the Arts Editor of *The Michigan Daily*. "John, you were waiting for my record review of **Abbey Road.**" He tossed a stapled collection of typewritten pages onto Gray's desk. "Well, you've got to read *this.*"

LaBour took a seat next to Gray and watched as the Arts Editor studied the manuscript. "Oh no, this is just too great!" Gray guffawed his way through the entire story without raising his eyes from it. "Is this your last class today, Fred?" Gray finally asked as he handed the pages back to the author.

"Yeah."

Gray looked LaBour straight into the eyes. "This is just too good to pass up, especially after the WKNR thing. I'm gonna bag everything else and give you a whole page of tomorrow's issue."

After class, the two journalists picked up a six-pack of beer from the Campus Corner convenience store and headed upstairs to the offices of *The Michigan Daily* to lay out the page for the next day's edition.

"Just how long did it take you to come up with this

masterpiece?" inquired Gray as he opened the door to the type-set department.

"It took about an hour and a half. It's the best bullshit I ever wrote and it only took an hour and a half."

The two laughed and then turned to the task at hand.

V.
"I Read The News Today, Oh Boy..."
—"A Day In the Life"
by the Beatles

Fresh stacks of the October 14 issue of *The Michigan Daily* sat in the racks beside the Hatcher Library, waiting for the early morning students. By noon, the newspaper was completely sold out. A second, and then a third press run soon followed suit. Academia ground to a halt as students passed around the newspaper to those who were not fortunate enough to get their own copies. An audio ambrosia of laughter, gasps and shuffling paper filled the classrooms. All of the attention was focused on the story on page 2, headlined: "McCartney Dead; New Evidence Brought to Light." It read as follows:

[EDITOR'S NOTE: Mr. LaBour was originally assigned to review *Abbey Road*, the Beatles' latest album, for the Daily. While extensively researching *Abbey Road*'s background, however, he chanced upon a startling string of coincidences which put him on the trail of something much more significant. He wishes to thank WKNR-FM, Louise Harrison Caldwell, and George Martin's illegitimate daughter Marian for their help. Mr. LaBour says it's all true. J.G.]

Paul McCartney was killed in an automobile accident in early November, 1966 after leaving EMI recording studios tired, sad and dejected.

The Beatles had been preparing their forthcoming album, tentatively entitled *Smile*, when progress bogged down in intragroup hassles and bickering. Paul climbed into his Aston-Martin, sped away into the rainy, chill night, and was found four hours later pinned under his car in a culvert with the top of his head sheared off. He was deader than a doornail.

Thus began the greatest hoax of our time and the subsequent founding of a new religion based upon Paul as Messiah.

The Beatles as a whole had considered seriously what would happen to them if one should meet with death as early as 1964 when substitute drummers were utilized to fill in

17

for an ailing Ringo Starr. However, it should be emphasized for the sake of religious records, that they had no definite premonition of the death of Paul. From all accounts, it appears to have been simply an unforeseen accident.

When word of Paul's untimely demise was flashed back to the studios, the surviving Beatles, in a hurriedly called conference with George Martin, decided to keep the information from the public for as long as possible. As John Lennon reportedly said, "Paul always liked a good joke," and it seemed that they considered the move an attempt to make the best out of a bad situation. As will be seen shortly, however, the "good joke" soon took on terrifying proportions.

George Harrison was called upon to bury Paul, Ringo conducted services, and John went into seclusion for three days. After his meditation, Lennon called another meeting of the group, again with George Martin, and laid the groundwork for the ensuing hoax. Lennon's plan was to create a false Paul McCartney, bring him into the group as if nothing had happened, and then slowly release the information of the real Paul's death to the world via clues secreted in record albums.

The plan was adopted, although Ringo expressed skepticism as to its possible success, and work began. (Brian Epstein was informed of the group's plan, threatened to expose it all, and mysteriously died, leaving five men who knew of the plot.)

First, a Paul Look-a-Like contest was held and a living substitute found in Scotland. He was an orphan from Edinburgh named William Campbell, and his picture can be found in the lower left-hand corner of the collage distributed with *The Beatles* album.

Minor plastic surgery was required to complete the image, and Campbell's mustache distracted everyone who knew the original McCartney from the imposter's real identity. The other Beatles subsequently grew mustaches to further integrate the "new" Paul into the group.

Voice print studies have confirmed the difference in voice timbre between the original and phoney Paul, but the difference was so slight that after studying tapes of Paul's voice and singing style, Campbell nearly erased entirely his own speech patterns and successfully adopted the late McCartney's.

Work then began upon the first post-Paul album, *Sergeant Pepper's Lonely Hearts Club Band. Smile,* incidentally, was junked and eventually picked up by Brian Wilson who attempted to salvage it but couldn't. He was allowed to work on *Smile* because the Beatles, especially Paul, had enjoyed "Good Vibrations" to a high degree and respected Wilson's ability immensely. *Smile* was finally thrown away and Capitol Records, ignorant of the whole plot, sued Wilson. Brian later paid tribute to Paul with *Smiley Smile*.

Lennon and Martin worked closely throughout the spring of 1967 on *Sgt. Pepper*. Their goal was an artistically and monetarily successful album filled with clues to Paul's death.

It was decided that an appropriate cover would include a grave and so it does. At the lower part of the grave are yellow flowers shaped as Paul's bass or, if you prefer, the initial "P." On the inside of the cover, on the fake Paul's arm, is a patch reading "O.P.D." which is a symbol used in England similar to our "D.O.A." meaning Officially Pronounced Dead. The medal upon his left breast is given by the British Army commemorating heroic death.

On the back cover, Paul's back is turned to us. The others are facing us.

The songs on the album contain numerous references to Paul's accident, "A Day in the Life" being the most obvious example. "A crowd of people stood and stared. They'd seen his face before...etc." When the top of a man's head is sheared off his identity is partially obscured.

The entire concept of the album, that of a different group, yet "one you've known for all these years" is significant.

Another facet of the plot is the emergence of Martin as an important composer, all the while masquerading as Paul. His old-time piano melodies, begun with "When I'm 64" and continuing through "Maxwell's Silver Hammer" are actually century-old barroom tunes he has extensively researched. If you recall, Martin has a scholarly background in all phases of music.

While *Sgt. Pepper* was being recorded, Lennon worked on a song called "Strawberry Fields Forever" and inserted at the end of the recording after the horn freakout, a distorted voice saying "I buried Paul." Play it at 45 rpm and check it out yourself.

"Strawberry Fields" eventually became incorporated into a larger work, *Magical Mystery Tour,* an album and film chocked full of veiled references to that rainy, tragic night.

Lennon had been doing a great deal of reading on the ritual of death in various cultures around the world (documented by Hunter Davies' authorized biography of the Beatles) and presented his knowledge graphically in *Tour*.

One instance is the constant appearance of a hand behind Paul's head in nearly every picture in the record album. The hand behind the head is a symbol to mystics of death. Another is the picture of Paul (Campbell) on page three with the poster saying "I YOU WAS" indicating change of identity. Another is the appearance of surgeons and policemen, both involved in Paul's car crash, on page five.

On pages ten and thirteen Paul is shown wearing black trousers and no shoes. Dead men are buried in black trousers and without shoes. Empty shoes, as appear next to Ringo's drums on page thirteen, were a Grecian symbol of death. And finally, on page 23 where the group has just descended a long, curving staircase, Paul is wearing a black rose while the other three are wearing red roses.

The songs again are paramount. "Magical Mystery Tour" implies the hoax in its entirety and marks Lennon's developing suspicion that the plot is out of hand. They are "dying" to take us away. "The Fool on the Hill" sits "perfectly still," as though dead, and grins a dead man's "foolish grin." On "Blue Jay Way" George Harrison, wrapped up in Eastern symbolism and religious fervor, implores Paul to resurrect himself before "very long" implying for the first time a realization of the essentially religious nature of the plot.

"Walrus" is Greek for corpse. John is "crying." He is also obviously contemptuous of those unaware of the plot, not having assumed the role of God he adopts later on. Also, the end of "Walrus" contains passages from King Lear about death and villains recorded simultaneously with the radio broadcast that never took place announcing Paul's death to the world. Played backwards, a favorite ploy of the Beatles as early as "Rain," the words "Paul's dead" can be plainly heard.

The closing song of the album, "All You Need is Love," lays the premises for Lennon's developing concept of his fledgling religion, with a tribute to Paul's early composing efforts at its conclusion coupled with his favorite old standard, "Greensleeves."

Before going on to *The Beatles* album, it should be explained more fully how the mechanics of hiding Campbell's identity were worked out. Before his death, Paul was a homosexual (as noted in "Yellow Submarine" when it is plainly yelled "Paul's a queer," answered by "Aye, aye, Captain"), so confused girlfriends were not a major problem for the plotters.

Paul rarely saw his only surviving parent anyway, and had had few close friends. Campbell was able to cover the part perfectly. It cannot be emphasized too heavily that Campbell is the primary reason for the success of the hoax. A girlfriend was needed to keep female admirers at bay, preventing infiltration or blackmail of the five men who knew of the plan so Peter Asher's sister Jane was paid a ripe sum to keep her mouth shut and pretend she was Paul's better half.

Last summer, of course, Campbell married a New York divorcee as Jane Asher was spirited out of sight and the plotters grew more confident of their substitute.

After *Magical Mystery Tour,* Campbell began playing a more prominent part in the actual realization of the plot. He was allowed to use his natural voice on "Lady Madonna" which many listeners thought was Ringo at first. This "tough guy" style of singing became integrated rapidly into the group and continued through to *Abbey Road.*

The Beatles appeared nearly a year ago with an all-white cover and hundreds of clues for the wary. The use of the white cover indicates Lennon's further adoption of a God-like image and an ever increasing sense of the value of purity of purpose to the plot.

The collage included with the album depicts Paul lying on his back in the upper left-hand corner, possibly deceased, in a pool of water, with the top of his head missing. As noted before, William Campbell's passport picture before joining the group is in the lower left-hand corner. The first song on the album, "Back in the U.S.S.R." is a thank-you note from the Beatles to Brian Wilson for his work on *Smile* and his cover-up job involving where the tapes originated.

"Dear Prudence" begs Paul to come back and "open up" his eyes. John called McCartney "Prudence" back in the old days when they were known collectively as the Nurk Twins. Nearly every tune on the album contains references to the hoax, culminating in Lennon's apocalyptic vision in "Revolution Number Nine."

This sound collage is clearly the whole story, according

to a God-like Lennon. Besides the obvious chaos, the "Take this brother, may it serve you well," the religious absolution and the eventual triumph of "Good Night," the tape played backwards near the beginning has a man saying "Turn me on, dead man," etc.

Thus we come to *Abbey Road*. (Monks live in abbeys.) On the cover is John Lennon, dressed in white and resembling utterly an anthropomorphic God, followed by Ringo the undertaker, followed by Paul the resurrected, barefoot with a cigarette in his right hand (the original was left-handed), followed by George the gravedigger.

And if you look closely, they have just walked out of a cemetery on the left side of the street. Thus, Paul was resurrected, given a cigarette, and led out of the tomb, thereby conquering death with a little help from his friends.

The real Paul is still dead, of course, but his symbolic resurrection works fine without him.

The album itself contains clues to his death and now, clues to his resurrection. "Maxwell's Silver Hammer" is a tale of religious justice, with a dashed-in head for punishment. "Octopus's Garden" is British Navy slang for the cemetery in England where naval heroes are buried. "I Want You (She's So Heavy)" is Lennon wrestling with Paul, trying to pull him out of the earth. Again John's apocalyptic vision has crystallized and after a seemingly endless amount of chaos and confusion, the music ends abruptly as Paul is extricated.

The second side announces the principles upon which the religion will be based: beauty, humor, love, realism, objectivity. It is a religion for everyday life. It analyzes interpersonal relationships in "You Never Give Me Your Money," explains Paul's part in the ritual in "Sun King" ("Here comes the sun king...Everybody's laughing..."), humorously, never cruelly, inspects money grubbers and fad followers in "Mean Mr. Mustard" and "Polythene Pam," and realistically looks at life with "Boy, you're gonna carry that weight a long time."

And at the end, Paul ascends to the right hand of John and proclaims, "the love you take is equal to the love you make."

But in the VERY end, they are joking about the Queen. The Beatles are building a mighty church, and when you emerge from it, you will be laughing, for Paul is the Sun of God.

"Outrageous," breathed Jonathan Newberry as he finished LaBour's article. Newberry was only one of the many students at the University of Michigan who were totally taken by the theory of McCartney's death. The satire in the *Michigan Daily* story was obvious, but there was something intangible about it that seemed to indicate a need for further investigation.

Newberry was sitting with a group of other students on the grass near the Science Department, just off of a common area called the "Diag" (which is criss-crossed diagonally by intersecting walkways). Among the circle of eight kids, there were only three newspapers to go around, so Beemy eagerly accepted his friend Newberry's copy.

"This guy LaBour is on target too often for this to be a lie," Newberry stated to no one in particular. "I mean, I always wondered what the O.P.D. on Paul's sleeve meant. Now I know."

"How did the guy figure this all out?" asked Beemy as he folded the paper and passed it to another in the group.

"It's nonsense," declared the girl seated next to Newberry, "the whole thing is a hoax. The writer ought to be ashamed of himself," she pouted.

"Yeah, right," Newberry responded dryly, "like you're some sort of expert. I saw you in the cafeteria last week reading *Naked Came the Stranger* by Penelope Ashe."

"So what?"

"So Penelope Ashe is a pseudonym for a bunch of guys who write for *Newsday*," Newberry knowingly revealed. "Now *that's* a hoax!"

Realizing that she had been ostracized, the girl picked herself up off the ground and dismissed the comment with a flip of her head as she walked away.

"Chicks don't have any sense," Beemy said to the now all-male group. "It's clear as day that something's going on...did any of you hear Uncle Russ last night?"

"I heard his show on Sunday," Newberry said, "but I

didn't really buy any of that crap until I read this." Newberry held the newspaper aloft. "LaBour tied it all together."

"Uncle Russ says that the Beatles are playing a game with us and that Paul probably isn't really dead," Beemy explained. "He thinks it's a way to test the perceptiveness of the public."

"I'll bet there's a lot more clues to be found," Newberry proposed, "and I'm gonna find them!"

Fred LaBour's *Michigan Daily* spoof turned out to be a major catalyst in the spread of the rumor. However, similar theories had already been spontaneously developing at other campuses across the country. By the time LaBour's article appeared on October 14, the "Paul-is-Dead" rumor was more than a month old at Ohio Wesleyan University.

VI.
"Nothing To Do To Save His Life"
—"Good Morning, Good Morning"
by the Beatles

The doorway to Professor Everett Haycock's sculpting class at Ohio Wesleyan University was jammed with students, most of whom did not even have an interest in the subject. Necks were craning and bodies were pushing to get a closer look at the real attraction: a handsome young man with a cascade of curly brown hair seated cross-legged on the center table. He was holding a copy of the Beatles' **Sgt. Pepper** album in his left hand, while pointing at the cover with his free hand.

"As you can see," the young man expounded, "Paul is the only member of the band with a raised hand above his head. We've discovered that this is a religious blessing to a dead man."

A chorus of surprised drawn breaths filled the classroom. The crowd pushed closer to the front as the dissertation continued.

"When you get home from classes today, pull out this album," he said, emphasizing the command by waving the Beatles' masterpiece over his head, "and look on the reverse side. You'll see that Paul is the only one not facing the camera and you'll ask yourselves the same question we asked: why is he being singled out on all of the albums?"

"Mr. John Summer," a voice called out from the back, "what in the hell is going on here?"

The curly-haired junior detective paused his demonstration and looked to the doorway to see Professor Haycock squeezing through the crowd toward him.

"Oh, hi, Professor. I guess it's time to sculpt." Summer hopped off the table and directed his next statement to the now-dissipating crowd. "See ya all tomorrow, same Bat Time."

John Summer was Ohio Wesleyan's in-house expert on the clues to McCartney's alleged death. Although he wasn't familiar with what was going on in Detroit, many of the clues in Summer's vast dossier were identical to those that were uncov-

JOHN SUMMER (CIRCA 1969)
Ohio Wesleyan junior John Summer heard about the rumor
at a back-to-school party, and spread the word to anyone who would listen.
(Photo courtesy John Summer.)

ered by Russ Gibb and Fred LaBour. It is important to mention here that, along with four fellow frat brothers, Summer had become acquainted with the rumor a month before the WKNR broadcast.

On a Friday night in September during the second week of classes, Summer, Jamie Reynolds, Bill Newman, Peter Sullivan and Jack Tucker were at a friend's apartment near the campus. As the beer flowed and the joints were passed, the cacophonous chatter of laughter and conversation blended into a warm friendly murmur.

"Hey, John!" Jamie Reynolds motioned Summer to come to the other side of the room. Picking himself off the floor where he had been sitting, Summer strolled over to where his friend was standing with someone he didn't recognize.

Reynolds took a gulp from his mug of Michelob and then directed his gaze at the stranger.

"John, this guy says Paul McCartney is dead!"

Summer grinned, raised his bottle of Robin Hood Ale, and took a deep swig. "Yeah, I know," he finally said, "He's hanging out in heaven with Bob Dylan."

"No, really," the stranger piped up, "that's all they're talking about at Drake University. McCartney died and the remaining Beatles are dropping hints about it on the records."

"Dropping hints? What are you going on about?"

"Do you have a copy of **Sgt. Pepper** around here? I'll show you."

The rest of the evening was spent discussing the "clues" on the cover of **Sgt. Pepper.**

And what happened at Drake University to cause all this excitement in Ohio? The story begins with a student named Dartanyan Brown. Also a struggling musician, Brown shared a residence with his band in Des Moines, Iowa. Their house also served as a commune of sorts for musicians who happened to be in town on tour. On any given night, one could find members of the Rotary Connection, Chicago Transit Authority, or Fuse camped out on the living room floor. The marijuana pipe and the bottle of Jack Daniels would make the rounds to anyone who wanted it and the conversation would continue until three in the morning.

During these rap sessions, the topic was invariably music-related. Brown's first week of classes at Drake did nothing to change that focus. On Friday night, he returned home from school to find the living room once again replete with an assortment of long-haired musicians and their girlfriends. One of Brown's roommates was quietly strumming out a chord pattern on an acoustic guitar while conversation bubbled around him.

Brown didn't recognize any of the people who visited the house that night, and he never saw them again. But when he returned to the Drake campus on Monday, he couldn't get one of the girls out of his mind. She had spent the entire evening talking about some supposed secret messages on Beatles albums and how they suggested Paul McCartney's death. The images that the girl had conjured utterly fascinated him.

Brown strolled into the office of the student newspaper, *The Drake Times-Delphic*, where he served as an associate editor. He discovered the bespectacled sports editor, Tim Harper, sitting alone and puffing thoughtfully on a cigarette.

After a dissertation from Brown, Tim Harper wasn't convinced that the Beatle was dead, but he thought that it would make a hell of a story for the *Delphic*. Harper's article, "Is Beatle Paul McCartney Dead?" appeared in the paper on Wednesday, September 17, 1969. It remains the earliest printed documentation of the rumor's existence on the college campuses of the United States.*

Meanwhile, back at Ohio Wesleyan, John Summer was elected among his friends to head an investigation team. They spent the rest of September scouring Beatles albums for clues.

---

*Less than a week later, on September 23, an article entitled "Something Wrong With McCartney? Clues Hint at Possible Beatle Death" appeared in the Northern Illinois University's *Northern Star*. The author, Barb Ulvilden, apparently got a hold of Harper's article and plagiarized him extensively, to the point of repeating his factual and grammatical errors. Ulvilden refuses to comment on her article.

The group was soon convinced that whatever they had stumbled upon would make a good news story, so Summer set out to sell the information to the wire services. Associated Press turned him down flat, indicating that they didn't buy stories—they sold them. He fared better with UPI, who agreed to put the story on the wire with his name as a source in case somebody was interested.

Quite a few people became very interested...

VII.
"O, Untimely Death!"
—The character Oswald,
from Shakespeare's *The Tragedy of King Lear*
[included in the Beatles' "I Am the Walrus"]

In America, the death of a hero has a powerful impact on our lives. Whether they come from the world of politics, the battlefield or the movie screen, our heroes have somehow made our existence more meaningful. They define our goals with their words and actions. They exude all of the traits that we'd like to find in ourselves: confidence, bravery, sexiness, intelligence. When we embrace our heroes, we embrace the ideal image of ourselves. And so it follows that when one of our heroes tragically perishes, we feel lost and alone.

President John F. Kennedy was such a hero to the younger generation. When this youthful and handsome visionary was violently slain, a void was left to fill. No charisma was found in Kennedy's successor. The time was ripe to find guidance outside of the political arena.

The Beatles first arrived on the American scene in early 1964 and they couldn't have timed it better. They looked different; they sounded fresh and vital. They wanted to hold our hand and we let them hold on tight for the next six years. The Beatles didn't offer any more than their music, but somehow we got so much more out of the deal. More than mere musicians, the Beatles were a unique cultural phenomenon. They influenced the length of our hair and the style of our clothing. They extolled the importance of peace, friendship and love. Even the business of making and selling record albums was changed forever.

With John, Paul, George and Ringo serving as the new breed of heroes, it was no surprise that so much attention was paid to the possibility that one of them might be dead. The mystery of Paul McCartney drew people together. If Paul was really dead, we would need each other's shoulder to cry on. If he was alive, we had to collectively get to the bottom of the matter.

On the day that Fred LaBour's story appeared in *The*

31

Michigan Daily, dozens of grieving students swamped the newspaper's office. Although it was obviously satirical in nature, the article's mere suggestion that Paul McCartney might no longer be among the living brought concerned teenagers from all over the campus. Through the tears, they asked whether it was true. The staff was amazed by this development; after all, the *Daily* had a history of publishing various outrageous items on its Arts and Entertainment page.

"It wasn't on page one, it wasn't 'This is news! Late-breaking story!'" LaBour explained recently. "We had all kinds of zany stuff we were doing with that page, so [my story] was completely in line with what we were doing."

Nevertheless, many students were genuinely concerned by the article's implication. Had McCartney become another fallen hero, or was this all a macabre hoax? The young generation needed to know and they began to search for the answer.

VIII.
"He Blew His Mind Out In A Car
He Didn't Notice That The Light Had Changed"
—"A Day in the Life"
by the Beatles

Wednesday, October 15, was Moratorium Day, a nation-wide deprecation of America's involvement in the Vietnam War. The holiday was marked by protests and rallies on campuses from coast to coast, and studies were virtually put on hold. At the University of Michigan, the get-togethers were well-attended, but in the wake of LaBour's article the previous day, hundreds of kids spent the afternoon in their dorms and apartments instead. They were busy dissecting Beatles albums.

"Eddie, take a look at what I found!" exclaimed Jonathan Newberry, as he handed the White Album giveaway poster to his roommate. "The *Daily* article doesn't mention anything about this."

Eddie put the smoldering joint that he had been smoking onto the edge of his desk. The twisted cigarette promptly teetered and fell to the hardwood floor. "Shit!" the stoned student roared as he killed the glowing tip of the roach with a well-placed shoe. He then reached for the poster and looked at the evidence in question. Among the montage of amateur photos of various Beatles, there was a full-length shot of McCartney, apparently laughing it up in the recording studio. But there was also something else in the photo and Eddie saw it immediately.

"Oh, wow," he gasped, pointing to a pair of shapes which seemed to be reaching out to grab the unaware musician, "those arms! They look like skeleton arms reaching out of the closet!"

Newberry was furiously writing away on his legal pad. "See? You see it, too! I'm gonna write a follow-up article on all these other clues that the *Daily* missed yesterday."

Eddie continued to be transfixed by this new troubling image. "Jonathan, the Beatles *really* are trying to tell us something about Paul. Why else would they put all this stuff in the pictures?"

"You don't need to convince me," Newberry responded,

"I've spent all morning digging up proof." He flipped back a few pages in his notes. "I want to know why the Beatles sing about 'carrying that weight' on the **Abbey Road** album. It's gotta be a coffin, don't you think?"

Eddie looked surprised and then pondered his roommate's remark for a moment. "Or," he proposed, "it could be the struggle of the band to carry on without Paul!"

"Good...good," Newberry said as he wrote Eddie's observations onto the pad. "And the song before that—'Golden Slumbers'—that's a long, long sleep."

"Of the dead," added Eddie.

"Right!"

"And 'The End'...well, that's *the end*."

Newberry smiled. "Eddie, you're definitely hip to this. You wanna co-author the article with me?"

"Nah. I got a sweet buzz on and I just want to give you my insight," Eddie said as he fired up another number.

Newberry's attention was suddenly drawn to a sight outside the window. "Hey, Fred!" he shouted to the two figures who had passed the dormitory. Fred LaBour and Jay Cassidy stopped and turned toward the voice and spotted Newberry.

"Fred, man, I want to tell you I loved your article." LaBour removed his eyeglasses from his shirt pocket and slipped them on. "Uh, thanks a lot," he shyly replied, "I just threw it together."

"Well, come on up and have a smoke. Let's rap about it."

LaBour shook his head. "No, thanks. Jay and I are heading down to the Moratorium rally at Burton Tower."

Flashing a thumbs-up, the student ducked back inside his dorm room, leaving the two friends to their journey.

As they proceeded toward the site of the demonstration, LaBour and Cassidy realized that the cacophony that they began to hear was not that of anti-Vietnam chants. Instead, familiar music met their ears as it wafted on the cool breeze from open windows.

"...Let me take you down," spoke one window as a second joined in with a chorus which sounded very much like "turn me on, dead man." Snatches of other Beatles songs—some backwards, some slowed-down—sang out to the amazed young men as they crossed the street and entered the Campus Corner convenience store.

The checkout line inside the shop snaked away from the register and around the canned foods aisle. A lone clerk rang and bagged six-packs of beer and record albums as two dozen kids impatiently waited to make their purchases. Excited murmuring was exchanged between the customers as Fred and Jay walked toward the beer cooler.

"Hey, LaBour!! I hope you didn't come here for brew," bellowed a student at the end of the line as he raised two cartons of Pabst skyward, "'cause I got the last of it!"

The beer cooler was indeed empty, as was the wooden bin that usually held an abundant supply of Beatles albums. As Fred LaBour absorbed all that he was witnessing, those students who had bought their "research materials" circled around him and asked questions about the *Daily* article. **Abbey Road** record albums were produced from brown bags and LaBour modestly responded to inquiries about Italian burial rites and cryptic song lyrics.

"The things you wrote about are so cool," exclaimed one girl. "Is it true Paul was killed at the same crosswalk that's on the front cover?"

Fred looked at Jay and laughed. "Yeah, that's right. The accident took place on Abbey Road and the Beatles are commemorating the tragedy. That's why the Volkswagen 'Beetle' is there."

"With Paul's age on the license plate," the girl deduced.

"Paul's age IF he had lived," LaBour corrected her.

"We were so turned on by your article," said a student who had bought three copies of **Abbey Road**, "that we didn't even get high at the dorm last night!"

LaBour wasn't sure whether he should say thanks or congratulations, so he simply nodded. "Well, look, we have to get going." He pushed through the crowd and waved to the students. "Keep searching, and ye will find."

The inquisition over, LaBour found himself back on the street with his friend.

"Man, oh man, Fred," commented Cassidy, "you're a celebrity. Everyone seems to recognize you."

LaBour smiled wryly. "You know, Andy Warhol once said that in the near future, everyone would be famous for fifteen minutes. I guess this is my Warholian Fifteen Minutes of Fame."

Although Fred LaBour didn't realize it at the time, his temporal allotment of fame was about to traverse the quarter-hour mark.

And the amazing thing was that it really hadn't even begun.

* * * * * * * * * *

Alex Bennett's weekly overnight talk show on WMCA was always a hotbed of opposing views. Every Saturday, thousands of New Yorkers tuned in to hear Alex introduce a new controversial topic and invite listeners to call in with their opinions. Occasionally, when subjects such as marijuana legalization were exhausted, the phone lines would be open to entertain discussion on just about anything—including rumors.

"Alex," one caller might offer, "this is George from Queens and I wanted to tell you and your listeners that Edward Armstrong didn't walk on the moon this past summer."

"Yes, that's true," Bennett might counter, "it was *Neil* Armstrong."

"Nobody walked on the moon. It was all staged by the government in the deserts of Arizona. They just want the Russians to think we're superior to them."

"Nice theory, pal," Bennett would say, "but how do you explain the photographs of the earth that were beamed back down to our television sets?"

"Alex," the caller would admonish, "you know all that stuff can be faked with cameras. They used a Rand McNally globe and put it into a Star Trek set with all those galaxies and —"

"Goodbye, sir. Thanks for the call."

On this Saturday, the eighteenth of October, the show

was supposed to be devoted to banter about the recent Moratorium, but because most of the callers opposed the U.S. involvement in Vietnam, the topic lost its controversial luster very quickly. Bennett opened up the phone lines to other issues and found an interesting topic on the first call.

"Alex, this is Lewis Yager and I'm a student at Hofstra University in Hempstead. I called to tell New York City that Paul McCartney of the Beatles is dead!"

Bennett cupped his hand over the microphone and turned to the news director. "Is there anything on the news wire about this?"

The newsman had already hurried over to the AP machine. Bennett removed his hand from the mike and proceeded with the call.

"Son, where did you get this information?"

"Well, three nights ago, my girlfriend called me at my dorm and told me that she had this horrible dream that McCartney died in a car crash and—"

"Wait a second—you mean this is all the product of a nightmare? It's just a rumor?"

Yager's voice took on an authoritative tone. "It's much more than a rumor. Here at Hofstra University, I have formed the 'Is Paul McCartney Dead Society' and we are determined to prove that he died three years ago in a car crash and the surviving Beatles have been telling us about it by placing clues on their record albums."

Bennett chuckled. When he was in college, it was goldfish-eating and telephone booth-stuffing that were the fads of the day. Now they're looking for secret messages on rock 'n' roll records. Bennett was about to dismiss Yager with a witty remark when he noticed that every one of his eight phone lines were winking their red eyes at him. He realized that this topic had already struck a nerve with his audience, so, still somewhat skeptical, he posed the inevitable question.

"What clues?"

IX.
"We Don't Often Sing Or Refer
To Death, I Don't Think So."
—John Lennon,
in a 1969 WKNR interview

In 1964, when Beatlemania first swept the United States, the subject matter of Lennon/McCartney compositions dealt primarily with love. However, as the Beatles and their audience matured, so did the songwriting. Other lyrical themes were explored by the band and some of these had a psychedelic edge which may have been the result of experimentation with mind-altering drugs. The obliqueness of some of these new lyrics certainly had a direct influence on the spread of the McCartney death rumor.

Beatle protests to the contrary, there are references to death in several songs. Although many of these are rendered with tongue-in-cheek posturing (such as "I'd rather see you dead, little girl, than to be with another man" in "Run For Your Life"), other references are more somber. For example, "She Said, She Said" (reportedly written by Lennon about actor Peter Fonda's remarks during a mutual LSD trip) has the central character repeating the assertion that "I know what it's like to be dead." And "In My Life" finds Lennon reflecting on his own existence—"With lovers and friends I still can recall/Some are dead and some are living."

Vagueness breeds free-association, and John Lennon, being the master of the obscure plume, offered an abundance of ambiguity. His lyrics were often open to individual interpretation and took on a myriad of meanings. Coupled with allusions to death were implications of the method—"He blew his mind out in a car" from "A Day in the Life" and "You were in a car crash/And you lost your hair" from "Don't Pass Me By" (actually credited to Ringo Starr, but most likely influenced by Lennon's penchant for weird couplets). One can readily see how a scenario of untimely death in an automobile accident may have been developed by imaginative fans. Although this does not explain the cause of the rumor itself, it most likely points to the source of some of the elaborate embellishments that gave the rumor palpability.

The cluesters took many of the death references out of context and applied them to the theory. Once again, the ambiguity of songs like "Good Morning, Good Morning" lent themselves to this intricate scrutiny: "nothing to do to save his life" is obvious, but the exploration of the automotive theme with "now you're in gear" was also considered as a definite "clue."

Why, asked the cluesters, was a Shakespearean death scene included in the fade-out to "I Am the Walrus"? *The Tragedy of King Lear* (Act IV, Scene VI) seemed to belie the playful words of the rest of the song. Here's the entire passage, as it appeared on September 29, 1967 on BBC's Third Programme, when the Beatles mixed the radio program live onto the master tape:

OSWALD: Slave, thou hast slain me:—villain, take my purse:
If thou wilt thrive, bury my body;
And give the letters which thou find'st about me
To Edmund Earl of Gloster; seek him out
Upon the British party:—O, untimely death!
[dies]
EDGAR: I know thee well: a serviceable villain;
As duteous to the vices of thy mistress
As badness would desire.
GLOUCESTER: What, is he dead?
EDGAR: Sit you down, father; rest you—

And, in the main body of "I Am The Walrus," the young sleuths saw more in the lyrics than simply a literary nod to Lewis Carroll and James Joyce. The "eggman" was a nickname for Humpty Dumpty and his fate was known to all—he fell and cracked his head open. From there, innumerable correlations between automobiles and death were drawn from every esoteric phrase in the song. To many of the cluesters, the song appeared to be John Lennon's account of his bandmate's fateful night.

The connection between automobiles and death extended beyond car crashes. It was surmised that an automobile was a symbol of spiritual travel; indeed, death was a Magical Mystery Tour that was "dying to take you away." Like pieces of an

immense and enigmatic jigsaw puzzle, abstract fragments somehow seemed to fit together to produce a complete picture.

But there were also cryptic lyrics that the cluesters felt
were concealed in some Beatles recordings and these were the
real proof that Paul was no longer among the living. John's
utterance that "I buried Paul" at the end of "Strawberry Fields
Forever" was the most obvious confirmation, but as the sleuths
dug deeper, other moribund allusions were revealed. "Paul
McCartney is dead, everybody! Really, really dead!" was found
beneath layers of music on "Sgt. Pepper's Reprise." When some
mysterious mumbling at the close of "I'm So Tired" was played
backwards, "Paul is a dead man, miss him, miss him, miss him"
was announced to shocked ears. And, of course, Russ Gibb and
his young caller Tom discovered the result of spinning "Revolution 9" in reverse: "Turn me on, dead man!"

The Beatles were fascinated with reversed sounds and
they were among the first to insert backwards sonic experi-
ments into rock songs. Witness the inverted guitar on "I'm Only
Sleeping" and the reversed speech on "Rain"; the Beatles unquestionably set a precedent that could serve as a device to hide
secret messages.

Backwards masking is a term coined to describe the process of placing reversed messages on record albums. There are
basically two categories of reversals: 1) the *engineered* reversal
and 2) the *phonetic* reversal. To achieve an engineered reversal,
a passage must be recorded normally and the tape then physi-
cally turned around. If this process is used with speech (as it
was on "Rain"), the result is usually garbled and indecipherable
as language. To reveal the original speech, the record or tape
must be played backwards. On "Rain," the backwards masking
was simply a line from the song—"When the rain comes, they
run and hide their head."

A phonetic reversal is a bit more complicated. If one takes
a phrase that sounds completely lucid in the forward motion
(e.g., the "number nine" recitation from "Revolution 9") and
spins it in reverse, it should sound nonsensical. On occasion,
however, an authentic-sounding English phrase may result by
pure coincidence (as when "number nine" becomes "turn me on,

dead man").

So all of the backwards clues to Paul's death are chance phonetic occurrences? Not necessarily. With practice, a person can learn to "speak backwards"; that is, a desired message such as "turn me on, dead man" can be recorded and then played backwards and an individual can learn the phonetic result. If the reversed version resembles another English-sounding phrase or an approximation thereof ("number nine"), then that phrase can be spoken forward onto the tape (with appropriate stressing and accent) and the consequence would be a deliberate phonetic reversal. The Beatles, therefore, may have placed "turn me on, dead man" in "Revolution 9" intentionally.

The other truly believable incident of reversed speech occurs at the end of "I'm So Tired." John Lennon utters something as the last guitar chord fades away. To many, when this mumbling is played in reverse, Lennon seems to be lamenting, "Paul is a dead man, miss him, miss him, miss him." If this is the case, then this would be an example of an *engineered reversal*.

In October of 1969, the cluesters uncovered other backwards messages. Most of these would fall under the phonetic reversal category and all of them are dubious at best. Nevertheless, the two convincing items cited above were enough to carry the weaker evidence and support the theory that hints of Paul's death were secreted in Beatles albums.

Along with the audio evidence, the "Paul-is-Dead" factions found compelling visual proof. The **Abbey Road** album cover contained a wellspring of data, most of which centered on death symbolism. Barefoot, Paul was said to be prepared as a corpse would be in Italy. A license plate on a Volkswagen "Beetle" announced Paul's age as "28 IF" he had lived. And the cluesters saw the procession across Abbey Road as that of a priest, an undertaker, a corpse, and a gravedigger.

A raised hand, thought to be the sign of divine benediction, was discovered above Paul's head in several photographs. It appeared once on the cover of **Sgt. Pepper's Lonely Hearts Club Band** and several times throughout the **Magical Mystery Tour** collection. Could it be mere coincidence that the same symbol of blessing appears so often? The cluesters didn't think so. Paul McCartney was obviously being singled out for a very specific reason.

And he was singled out in other ways as well. He's the only Beatle with his back turned toward the camera on the reverse sleeve of **Sgt. Pepper.** He's the only Beatle sporting a black carnation in a photograph from the **Magical Mystery Tour** booklet (black flowers are rare and considered unlucky). And he's the only Beatle out of step on the cover of **Abbey Road.** To those who believed in the rumor's validity, these items had to be more than random events.

Interpretation of many of the "clues" may have stretched credulity; however, it isn't difficult to comprehend how the aggregate theory came to be. Some of the evidence is believable and, besides, John Lennon had informed the public that there were clues to be found. In the song "Glass Onion," released a year before the controversy, he sings: "Well, here's another clue for you all/The walrus was Paul." Now, how much more explicit can one be?

* * * * * * * * *

"A guy in my folklore class told me that when Nordic Vikings started off on a journey to hunt food and encountered a dead walrus on the way, they would turn back. It was bad luck."

John Summer nodded in response to Jack Tucker's statement and jotted the words into his notebook. "Yeah, I heard about that. What about—"

The telephone rang through Summer's question. "Here we go again," he said as he smiled and reached for the receiver. Ever since the notice appeared on the UPI news wire, it was common for the proceedings at John Summer's campus apartment to be interrupted by calls from the press. Dozens of journalists throughout the nation had contacted Summer for interviews and he happily provided details of the theory to every newspaper and radio station that called. He was now speaking with a reporter from the *Delaware Ohio Gazette.*

"That's right," Summer said to the reporter, "if McCartney

is not dead, someone is trying to give the impression that he is dead." Those assembled at the apartment sat cross-legged at Summer's feet, listening and agreeing with every statement that their spokesman gave. "I'd say we started our research on a Friday in September," Summer continued, "and brought our findings to UPI just last week...yes, we're sure about all of this."

After the interview, Summer sat back down on the floor. "Well, we're getting publicity, but no hard cash. Nobody seems to be buying interviews."

"Who cares?" interjected Tucker, "This is a groove. Who needs to get paid for it?"

Back in Ann Arbor, Michigan, Fred LaBour initially felt the same way. His phone, too, had been ringing nonstop for the past week and the attention from the media thrilled him. He responded to the questions put to him with bravado, defending the validity of his "news story." When Joel Clark of *The Grand Rapids Press* contacted him and asked whether the article was serious, LaBour insisted that "it's on the level, man." (He also told Clark that his life's ambition was to be a commercial fisherman somewhere in Alaska).

However, by the time the calls began to come in from New York and London, he became overwhelmed. Fred began to tell the callers that Mr. LaBour had gone into seclusion and he couldn't be reached. The endless ringing of the telephone finally did drive him into exile and he moved to his girlfriend's home.

When LaBour briefly returned to his apartment to retrieve a few of his textbooks for class, the phone naturally rang out before he had a chance to leave. Reaching for the receiver, he thought to himself, "I'll just tell them that it's all a joke. Then they'll leave me alone."

"Hello?"

"May I speak with Mr. LaBour, please?"

"If this is about my article in *The Michigan Daily*—"

"Why, yes," the female voice responded, "I'm calling from RKO Film and Television. How would you like to be on a television special?"

X.

"There's So Much Evidence That It Couldn't Be Coincidental. I Believe Paul's Dead."

—Pat Rogalski, 16, a student from West Tech High
(as told to the *Cleveland Plain Dealer*)

"Paul?"

The Beatle immediately recognized the voice on the phone. Remaining seated on the mahogany piano bench, he pivoted away from the keyboard and shifted the receiver to his left ear. "What's up, Derek?"

"Listen, Paul," Derek Taylor proceeded, "there's this rumor about you going on in the States. Some deejay is saying that you're dead."

"Well, I'm not, mate. Don't even feel under the weather."

"Paul," the press agent continued, "they're saying that you've been dead for three years and that a double is standing in for you."

"Splendid," McCartney chuckled, "then *he* can deal with John."

"This isn't a joke, Paul."

"What's the hang-up? It'll fade quickly enough."

"I thought the same thing myself last week," Taylor sighed, "but now it's getting out of hand. The Apple offices have been deluged with inquiries concerning your whereabouts..."

"Well, they can keep on inquiring," the Beatle interrupted, "because I'm not leaving St. Johns Wood to come to Apple, if that's what you have in mind. The album's done and I'm taking a break. Linda and I are trying to raise a family."

"Paul, if you would just call the press in London or New York and make a statement—"

"No. In fact, I sort of fancy the idea." A smile crept across the musician's face. "It reminds me of James Dean—a young man, full of promise, cut down in the prime of his life."

"This is really not a time for adolescent fantasies."

"Being a Beatle is an adolescent fantasy," McCartney asserted, "and I'll do as I see fit. Look, Derek—don't worry about it. This is just one of those silly rumors. It'll fizzle in a couple of

45

days. In the meantime, tell them the truth. I want to be left in peace with my family."

Satisfied that that was the end of the matter, McCartney bid farewell to Taylor and resumed his work at the piano.

* * * * * * * * * *

A first generation American born of Scottish immigrant parents, Russ Gibb knew what it meant to work hard in order to earn a piece of the pie. When he wasn't teaching high school English or spinning progressive rock on WKNR, Gibb could usually be found at one of the three nightclubs that he owned and operated around the Detroit area. The Grande Ballroom, the largest and most successful of these venues, often featured live performances by such rock 'n' roll luminaries as Cream and Bob Dylan. Tonight, however, the bill of fare would be a young guitar-heavy outfit that had been born out of the ashes of The Pack.

The Pack was a local favorite in the cities of Flint and Detroit. Although they made a minor chart appearance with "I (Who Have Nothing)," little materialized for the band in the way of a national hit single. The Pack called it quits and leader Terry Knight went back to his previous vocation of radio announcing. He did, however, find the time to cut a solo single for Capitol Records in the spring of 1969, but the record didn't even crack the Top 100. Immediately afterwards, Knight persuaded a couple of his former bandmates to join him in a new venture. Having coaxed bassist Mel Schacher from Question Mark and the Mysterians to join guitarist Mark Farner and drummer Don Brewer, Knight dubbed them Grand Funk Railroad and became their promoter, producer and business manager.

Tonight at the Grande Ballroom, Grand Funk would begin its first national tour, riding high on the success of a debut album. Gibb watched the band set up their equipment as he sipped continuously from a can of Coca-Cola. Farner and Brewer laughed at something Terry Knight said, while Schacher seemed absorbed instead with the tuning of his bass guitar. Gibb strolled across the empty dance floor, carefully avoiding the snakes of audio cable that slithered toward the sound board. As he approached the stage, Knight spotted him and extended his hand outward.

"Russ Gibb, the pleasure's mine," said Knight, as he firmly shook the proprietor's hand. "This is a real fine place you've got here."

Gibb glanced around himself. "Yeah, I think it'll be big enough for all your fans."

"For now," Knight replied with a grin, "but the hype I've got in store for the band will make Shea Stadium too small for the audience." Knight took a seat on the edge of the stage and motioned Gibb to do the same. "This is it for me. I couldn't make it as a disc jockey. I couldn't make it as a musician—you didn't even play my single on WKNR, did you?"

Gibb shrugged his shoulders. "I never heard it, but we still play the stuff you did with the Pack."

"Grand Funk Railroad," Knight stated, "will probably never get played on the radio either, but the kids love us. You'll see that tonight. The new album is almost gold already and it's only on a few playlists across the country. Word of mouth does wonders."

Gibb nodded in agreement, but his thoughts turned toward the McCartney rumor. Word of mouth *does* do wonders, especially for the ratings of a tiny unknown FM radio station and its weekend disc jockey. It had only been a week since Gibb had discussed the rumor on his radio show and he already saw the ratings soar. Newspapers had been calling him all weekend for interviews and information. "I'm going to milk this for all it's worth," thought Gibb. "Terry Knight doesn't have the copyright on self-promotion."

After the Grand Funk Railroad concert got underway, Gibb was on the telephone to Dan Carlisle, and the two decided to team up with fellow deejay John Small to produce a documentary on the rumor. Within the hour, all three men were sequestered in the WKNR production studio, intent upon creating a ninety-minute special that would cover all aspects of the McCartney mystery. Transatlantic phone calls were placed to the London Apple offices in an effort to secure an interview with the elusive musician. Records were played at every speed and in every direction conceivable in order to produce the various "clues" that had been mentioned by listeners in the past week. And "experts" were consulted to confirm the religious symbolism of Paul's bare feet.

As night became morning, the disc jockeys continued to work. Carlisle had just transferred the song "Your Mother Should Know" onto reel-to-reel tape when Gibb entered the cluttered production studio.

"Danny, do you know what a glass onion is?"

Carlisle didn't look up from the tape machine as he spooled a tape onto the take-up reel, but his voice indicated an intense interest. "You mean like in the song?"

Gibb took a seat next to his comrade and let out a heavy sigh. "It took me eight hours on the telephone to find out what a goddamn glass onion is. I had calls to Oxford University, the Webster Dictionary folks, some guy in the offices of—"

"Well, go on," Carlisle interrupted as he turned his attention away from the tape player, "what *is* a glass onion?"

Gibb stared straight into Carlisle's eyes. "You won't believe it. Supposedly, it's an old British slang term for casket handles. Instead of metal handles, the eighteenth century British coffins had a glass ball that you would use to carry them."

"And if you're in the coffin," Carlisle continued the line of reasoning, "you could be looking through a glass onion!"

"Right. And is Paul looking out 'to see how the other half lives'?"

"Outrageous!" Carlisle exclaimed.

Gibb glanced up at the studio clock. "Hell, it's two in the morning! I've got a class to teach tomorrow." As he stood to leave, Carlisle clasped a hand on the man's shoulder and gently eased him back into his chair.

"Oh no, Russ," Carlisle scolded as he switched on the tape machine. "First, you're going to hear what *I've* been working on for the last couple of hours."

An ethereal droning sound filled the studio as Carlisle explained the experiment he had conducted. "This is 'Your Mother Should Know.' The entire song is playing backwards and the

Beatles are singing about God and death."

Gibb felt a chill run through his body as he listened to something that sounded like a Gothic wail. Maybe he was just tired, but he could swear that he was hearing phrases such as "I shed the light" and "why doesn't she know me dead." Up to this point, Gibb was simply using the rumor as a promotional tool, not imagining for a moment that there was any truth to it. But now he was beginning to experience some strange feelings.

He listened again. Yes, he was quite sure he heard it. Hidden in the reversed music track were voices singing "I shed the light...why doesn't she know me dead." Surely, the Beatles had placed the phrases in the song on purpose. Gibb turned toward Carlisle and, in an audibly shaken voice, posed the question that was uppermost in his mind.

"Danny, do you think he's *really* dead?"

XI.
"Paul Died In An Earthquake In Mexico In 1967. My Daughter Has Been Standing In For Him Ever Since."
—Mike McGear (Paul's brother)
in a quip to UPI London.

One of the most captivating aspects of the "Paul-is-Dead" theory was the idea that a double had taken McCartney's place in the group. The most widely-accepted account had the Beatles holding a McCartney Look-Alike Contest shortly after the auto accident. The winner, an Edinburgh orphan named William Campbell, was spirited away to a secret Beatle hideout and meticulously trained to assume the role of the deceased musician. Not only did Campbell bear a striking physical resemblance to Paul, he possessed a voice and knowledge of music that made the switch seemingly imperceptible. William Campbell, in effect, became Paul McCartney with comparative ease.

The existence of William Campbell can be traced directly to the article written by Fred LaBour. "I made up the guy," LaBour boasted recently. "It was originally going to be 'Glenn Campbell', with two N's and then I said 'that's too close, nobody'll buy that', so I made it William Campbell."

A little-known fact was that there *was* a Paul McCartney Look-Alike Contest held in the U.S. in 1966, and LaBour used this information as a basis for his fiction: "There had been Keith, if you remember, he had won [the contest]."

Keith (Philadelphia-born James Barry Keefer) entered the contest sponsored by an American teen publication and finished in first place. After his victory, Keith signed with Mercury Records, where he enjoyed two hit singles, the most successful being "98.6" in 1967.*

---

*Derek Taylor, during a WKNR interview with Russ Gibb, mentioned another Keith—British singer and emcee Keith Allison—as the winner of *Sixteen* magazine's McCartney look-alike contest. Neither "Keith" looked very much like Paul, and their records prove they didn't sound like him either.

The concept of a double for McCartney was not an unusual one in a society that has always been intrigued by such a notion. The widely-held belief that there is an identical but unrelated twin to every person on earth has been an element of Western civilization since the time of the Roman Empire. The Germans, in fact, even have a word for it: *doppelganger*. It is, therefore, not entirely incomprehensible why the public wholeheartedly endorsed the idea of a McCartney imposter.

Nevertheless, in keeping with the thesis that the Beatles wished to tip off the public to the ruse, the cluesters claimed that there was visual evidence that Paul was not Paul. They pointed to a facial scar above "Paul's" lip on a photograph from the "White Album." The pre-1966 Paul never had such a deformity, claimed the sleuths. Additionally, every Beatlemaniac knew that Paul was a lefty and, yet, the "Paul" on the cover of **Abbey Road** had a cigarette poised in his right hand!

Some of the songs credited to Paul McCartney also seemed to indicate that something was amiss. The voice on the song "Oh! Darling"—advertised as that of McCartney—sounded entirely different from the dulcet tones of "Yesterday." "Lady Madonna," initially mistaken by many as a Ringo Starr vocal, didn't sound like McCartney either. The cluesters were sure these subtle hints were intentionally planted so that keen observers could discover the truth.

Naturally, denials came fast and furious from Beatleland. Derek Taylor, the group's publicist, repudiated the doppelganger theory and Iain MacMillan (photographer for the **Abbey Road** sleeve) told the Associated Press that "if it's a double and not the real Paul, it's a very talented double."

Legal experts pointed out that an imposter would have a very difficult time trying to convince the British government that he was Paul McCartney. It was documented that Paul had recently received a new passport (which would require his fingerprints) and had been issued a marriage certificate on March 12, 1969, when he wed Linda Eastman. Most cluesters didn't accept this argument because, they surmised, the Beatles had enough money to purchase the cooperation and silence of anyone they desired.

Bruce Cook, a writer for the *National Observer*, found the hypothesis of a double preposterous and jested that "if Paul McCartney really did die shortly before the group recorded **Sgt. Pepper** and opened all those new horizons in pop, then they had better stick with this new guy and quit dropping all those dumb hints that he's not genuine. He's better than genuine. He's a distinct improvement."*

---

*"Around and Around Go the Rumors," by Bruce Cook, *National Observer* (October 27, 1969)

XII.
"I Was Alone, I Took A Ride, I Didn't Know What I Would Find There..."
—"Got to Get You Into My Life"
by the Beatles

Jay Cassidy's beat-up Corvair wheeled onto the interstate. "Green River" by Creedence Clearwater Revival issued from the car radio as Cassidy and Fred LaBour kept the beat by rhythmically rapping on the dashboard. The two young men were on the way to Metro Airport where LaBour would board a morning flight to Los Angeles. He had agreed to participate in the production of a "Paul-is-Dead" TV program hosted by the famed attorney F. Lee Bailey. LaBour wasn't exactly sure why he had allowed himself to be persuaded, but it was too late to change his mind now.

As John Fogerty's growl faded away on the radio, the baritone of Russ Gibb took over. "Well, gang...that was C.C.R. and that does it for me today...I'm on the way to the airport to leave the chill of the Motor City...to the sun of California...gonna do a TV show about this Paul McCartney mystery..."

"Hey, Uncle Russ is going to be there, too!" Cassidy beamed.

"Shhhh!"

"I'll keep all you people informed," Uncle Russ continued, "about the date...and time it will be aired...maybe we'll get to the bottom of this whole thing...see ya next week."

As the first chords of a new Bob Seger System song punched out over the air, Cassidy could see that his friend was deep in thought. For the next few miles, they rode without conversation until LaBour's face finally broke out in a small but obvious smile. He reached into his pocket and pulled out the American Airlines ticket that he had picked up the day before.

"Take my ticket, Jay," he said as he offered the envelope. "You go in my place!"

Cassidy looked down at the envelope and then returned a disappointed sneer to his passenger. "I don't understand—are you going chicken on this whole deal?"

"You're right," LaBour countered, "you *don't* understand.

Can't you see? This death hoax is all a gag, so why don't we turn my TV appearance into a gag? *You* go as *me!*"

The sneer on Cassidy's face metamorphosed into an amused grin. As he stifled a burst of laughter, he blurted out a choked but emphatic "Yeah!!"

"Imagine," LaBour continued as he made grand sweeping gestures with his hands, "we'll put one over on the whole world! There you'll be, grinning away, knowing that we out-hoaxed the hoax. Nobody but our families and friends will know the real story."

The Corvair left the highway, taking the ramp that led to Metro Airport. A short-term parking space was found and the car's engine became silent. Detroit's early morning fog was burning off and the immense grey bodies of 727s could be seen lumbering onto the runway. The two figures in the Corvair sat and talked, but neither left the car for several more minutes. Finally, one of the men stepped out, waved to the other and walked to the terminal.

Having reconsidered that he'd hoaxed enough for one lifetime, Fred LaBour boarded his flight and was on the way to Los Angeles.

* * * * * * * * * *

Enigmatic mysteries require equally enigmatic methods by which to solve them. The famous seeress Jeane Dixon (whose claim to fame was the prediction of JFK's assassination) was up for the task and conducted a seance to find out whether Paul was alive or dead. "People from all over the United States and England have been calling me about Paul McCartney," she told the *Philadelphia Inquirer*. "[He] is still alive and playing with the Beatles," she claimed.

Despite Dixon's metaphysical assurance, Lewis Yager and his *Is Paul McCartney Dead Society* at Hofstra University continued to gather evidence to the contrary. *Life* magazine, always with an eye on developing social movements, caught wind of Yager's unusual campus club and sent reporter John Neary to the small Hempstead, New York college.

Yager eagerly pulled out his file folder and went over the various clues with Neary. There was Paul in the **Magical Mystery Tour** album booklet, seated behind a sign which read: "I WAS." On another page in the same booklet, a cartoon drawing of Paul held a toy car. "That," explained Yager to the reporter, "is a model of the automobile McCartney perished in."

On the next page was a photograph of the Beatles in the midst of a performance. Yager pointed to McCartney's feet. "Barefoot. Just like on the cover of **Abbey Road**." His finger glided across the page until it came to rest upon two objects next to the bass drum. "And here we have his shoes...stained with blood!" Yager said dramatically.

Neary squinted at the photograph and saw that there was some red coloration on the otherwise brown shoes. "Couldn't that just be printing run-off?"

"Nope. It's blood. See how it's broken up in droplets?"

"Very convincing," Neary finally agreed.

Yager picked up the **Sgt. Pepper** album and opened up the gatefold. "Inside here, we have Paul wearing an arm-patch with the initials O.P.D. on it. 'Officially Pronounced Dead,' as our British friends in the medical field would say."

Yager next led the reporter over to a small hi-fi system and placed the first side of the **Abbey Road** album onto the turntable. As the song "Come Together" filled the tiny dorm room, the student sleuth began to decipher the oblique lyrics for Neary.

"First, Lennon sings 'he wear no shoeshine'," Yager shouted over the music, "and we can plainly see that Paul is barefoot on the front cover; he wouldn't need any shoeshine. Second, there's the line 'he got monkey finger'. Now, what does that make a person do?" Yager asked the reporter. When Neary shrugged, Yager snatched the **Abbey Road** cover from the reporter's hands and stabbed a finger at the image of McCartney. "It makes a person look at Paul's hands, doesn't it? And we don't see a 'monkey finger', whatever that is. But what we *do* see is a cigarette—in Paul's right hand. McCartney is left-handed!"

The audio discovery on "Revolution 9," however, was Yager's proudest accomplishment. Giving a copy of his notes to the *Life* reporter, Yager explained how he had recorded the entire selection backwards and was able to decipher a car crash, crackling flames, screams, car horns, and a mysterious monologue:

> He hit a light pole and we better go to see a surgeon. So, anyhow, he went to see a dentist instead who gave him a pair of teeth which wasn't any good at all...My wings are broke and so is my hair...I'm not in the mood for words. Find the night watchman...A financial imbalance...Must have gotten it between the shoulder blades.

"This is really wild," Neary expressed. "What else did you find in the song?"

"There's actually a negative clue in 'Revolution 9' near the end," Yager replied as he pulled a sheet from his file. "A woman's voice can be heard under a man's groans and she says, quote: 'Maybe he not dead...maybe he isn't dead.' But, see, it's not definitive."

Neary was impressed and he assembled the data for a future article in *Life*. He asked Yager if the Society really thought McCartney was dead. "We originally thought he was dead," Yager told the reporter, "but we decided that was too emotional. We all ought to sit back and analyze this rationally."*

---

*"The Magical McCartney Mystery," by John Neary, *Life* (November 7, 1969).

XIII.
"I Heard The Radio The Other Day/
I Heard Something That Blew My Mind"
—"So Long, Paul" by Jose Feliciano
(recording as Werbley Finster)

WABC, the powerful New York AM station, was known in the heyday of Beatlemania as "W A Beatle C." Capitalizing on the attention directed toward the group's first visit to America, the station rode it for all it was worth. The temperature was announced in "Beatle degrees" and new promotional contests were conducted nearly every day. By additionally featuring exclusive interviews with the Fab Four, WABC turned the Beatles' success into their own and generated the highest ratings in the city. It therefore comes as a great surprise that, five and a half years later, WABC chose not to use the McCartney rumor to its benefit.

Rick Sklar, then station manager, was not amused when he heard overnight disc jockey Roby Yonge discussing the rumor during his October 21 shift. "We'll get to the bottom of this," Yonge assured his listeners, as Sklar rushed to the station to yank the jock off the air.

"He was discussing [the rumor] incoherently," Sklar explained the next morning to UPI. "He wasn't with it and didn't sound like himself."

Sklar felt that focusing air time on the death rumor would hurt the station's image, so he had issued a directive to that effect. Yonge, however, could not resist the inherent publicity for himself and he chose to ignore the ban. He was fielding phone calls when Sklar arrived. Yonge looked up from the phone banks and saw his boss through the studio glass. Instead of barricading himself in the broadcast booth—as Sklar imagined he might—the renegade deejay simply relinquished his chair to a substitute jock and peacefully allowed himself to be escorted out of the building. Because his contract was due to expire in less than two weeks anyway, Yonge was summarily dismissed. He never set foot inside the station again.

Despite the muzzle at WABC, most of the radio stations

throughout the country welcomed discussion about the rumor. In fact, some stations actually encouraged their on-air personalities to carry on about it. It was good publicity for a station trapped in the ratings cellar. This was especially true in the case of FM outlets.

In 1969, Frequency Modulation (FM) radio was still considered an industry plaything, and AM was where the audience and money were. It was then only very recently that FM had found a market of sorts with an underground rock format developed by Tom Donahue at KSAN. The idea behind Donahue's format was to play album cuts instead of the hits and then rap about the philosophies behind the songs. Underground radio was adopted by several FM stations, including WKNR in Detroit, and it seemed to be gaining an audience. In the waning days of the sixties, however, an FM station's revenue paled beside its big AM sister, and this led many of the outlets to take chances in order to gain exposure. It would not be too farfetched to suggest that this situation played an important role in the dissemination of the McCartney rumor.

The AM outlets, nonetheless, were also keen on the controversy. Bill Gavin, editor of the industry newsletter *Top Forty*, surveyed the top stations and found the majority had covered the story as serious news, and that many had done full-length specials on the rumor. "The thing about this is it's got staying power," wrote Gavin.

"It doesn't matter whether it's true or not," KLEO deejay Alvin Davis told *Rolling Stone* magazine, "it's still entertaining. We've really got a lot of people talking about it."

Radio stations from New Orleans (WTIX) to New York (WNEW) watched their ratings soar after they presented "Paul-is-Dead" specials. Even WPLJ in New York enjoyed success with a program that ridiculed the rumor-mongers. In the show, entitled "Think For Yourself," announcer Bob Lewis spent an hour debunking the accumulated evidence. An excerpt:

> LENNON (from "A Day In the Life"): I read the news today, oh boy...

> LEWIS: And the news was full of it, man. Full of clues,

60

that is, to the death of Paul McCartney. And you could prove it if you could find the right things to look at on their albums. For example, the cluesters say that on the front of the **Sgt. Pepper** album, the Beatles are all standing facing Paul. Well, as a matter of fact, they're not...okay? It's as direct as that. Now, the other Beatles *do* have their bodies turned towards Paul. That hardly seems any indication that Paul is dead.

Other stations also remained sober in their discussions about the rumor. A disc jockey from WEBN-FM, an underground station in Cincinnati, read from a copy of Fred LaBour's *Michigan Daily* article and then tossed it aside. "We have concluded that there are people who want to believe that Paul McCartney is dead, but it isn't true," the jock told his audience. "We would really appreciate nobody calling us with your further theories because, frankly, we've had enough of this. I don't care if Paul McCartney is dead or not, as long as the Beatles keep putting out the music, which is my contact with them. Okay? That's the end of it."

But, for the most part, the airwaves were extremely receptive to the needs of the audience. Radio stations became electronic taverns for meeting with fellow cluesters and drinking up new information. Many disc jockeys opened up the phone lines to allow listener participation and often found the response to be overwhelming. The "Paul-is-Dead" rumor was the hottest hit on the dial.

WSAI-AM in Cincinnati put together a "Paul-is-Dead" special and invited John Summer and his friends to participate. They sat in the studio with the deejay and spent the first half of the show debating the validity of some of the clues:

> WSAI DEEJAY: I noticed you started pointing out the medal on McCartney's left breast. However, Harrison has the same medal. So if this is really, as I've heard, a medal for dying heroically, then why does [Harrison] have it? I would suggest that maybe that's the medal for the House of Lords that they won, remember? That OBE medal?

Despite the deejay's skeptical tone, he also believed that

the Beatles were behind the discovered clues. "We do not believe that Paul McCartney is dead," he said as he closed the show. "Neither do we believe that the Beatles are laying the foundation for a worldwide organized religion. The past three days at WSAI should teach us all a lesson. If you're still trying to solve the Beatles puzzle, think about this: doesn't it all fit together *too* well?

"We think we've all been had. We think it's a grand practical joke...a three-year, history-making punch line. The Beatles, we believe, have schemed to let us out-clever ourselves with all our mystic interpretations and abstract deductions. *Touche!*

"We think the Beatles are accusing us of taking ourselves too seriously. And if that's the case, we think they're right."

At WNEW in New York, Christopher Glenn wrote, produced and voiced a "News Close-Up" on the rumor. Glenn avoided the same kind of sensational program that was being offered by hundreds of other outlets and instead kept his show focused on the rumor as a sociological phenomenon. "Is Paul McCartney dead?" Glenn asked after presenting some of the clues. "I don't think so. Paul McCartney doesn't think so. But there is, or appears to be, a considerable body of evidence that he is. The whole business is fun, right? But there's more to it than that."

Glenn then presented Dr. Stanley Milgrum, a sociologist from the City University of New York. Dr. Milgrum explained to Glenn and the radio audience that the two elements that underlie the development of a rumor were ambiguity and importance. If a situation contained ambiguity (such as the clues from the records) and was important to people (what could be more vital than the Beatles?), then there would be a fertile breeding ground for myth.

When would the rumor burn itself out? "It may reach its peak, perhaps at about Easter time," Dr. Milgrum speculated, "because then the whole issue of whether an important figure is alive or dead comes to the fore of many people. The whole question of resurrection comes to the fore. So that would be a natural peaking point where, at that time, people will not say McCartney is dead, but that he has risen."

WMCA in New York saw the ratings potential and decided to capitalize on it. To that end, talk show host Alex Bennett was dispatched to London. It was his mission to seek out the missing Beatle and bring audio evidence back to the station. In the first few days, Bennett was unable to locate McCartney, but he collared an amazing cast of character witnesses instead. For instance, Bennett managed to track down McCartney's official barber who happily stated that Paul's slightly defective part in his hair was the same now as it had been in 1966.

Ringo Starr, in the middle of filming "The Magic Christian" with Peter Sellers, took a few moments to talk with Bennett:

BENNETT: What can you say to dispel these rumors that have started in the United States?

RINGO: I can't say anything, you know. I can only say that it's not true...No matter what I say, people won't believe it.

Ringo was correct. No amount of nay-saying could assuage the masses. When Paul McCartney himself finally decided to make a statement, it also fell on deaf ears.

XIV.
"When You Were Stoned, You Could Always Find Clues...But You Could Also Find Them When You Were Straight..."
—An alumnus from Ohio State University

After six whirlwind years with the Beatles, Paul McCartney was beginning to settle down. He found domestic bliss as a husband to Linda and a father to Heather and Mary. There was a change in McCartney's personal life, and this presaged a change in his professional life as well. With **Abbey Road** on the charts and the "Get Back" sessions undergoing a face-lift through the able hands of stellar producer Phil Spector, there was finally time for all of the Beatles to sit back and reflect on their careers.

Paul loved being a Beatle, but in his heart he knew that it was all coming to an end. It was time to begin anew and Paul initiated the process symbolically by going into seclusion. The real reason, however, for his public withdrawal was a desire to record a solo album in his home studio, a place where he could be both an artist and a family man.

When McCartney first caught wind from Derek Taylor that there was a rumor about his death, he refused to make a public denial. Not realizing the consequence of his silence would be an escalation of speculation, McCartney originally found the notion of his secret death to be amusing. He recalled a similar rumor about Ringo Starr that made the rounds in 1965 when the Beatles toured the South Pacific with drummer Jimmy Nichol in tow. In truth, Ringo was back in London, suffering a bout of tonsillitis. The rumor was quashed rather quickly and McCartney was sure that would be the case with the "Paul-is-Dead" stories.

A week had passed since Taylor called, but the rumor hadn't dissipated; in fact, it had grown stronger and more focused. When Paul heard something about "clues" on record albums, he decided he had to make some sort of statement.

Paraphrasing Mark Twain—who encountered a similar problem over sixty years before—Paul said: "I am alive and well and unconcerned about the rumors of my death. But if I were dead, I would be the last to know." Because he was still intent upon protecting his privacy, he issued his quote to the Apple press representatives instead of calling a proper press conference. Although the statement appeared in dozens of newspapers on Wednesday, October 22, the kids weren't buying it. After all, said the cluesters, why didn't Paul make the statement first-hand via television or radio? Did he have something to hide?

Russ Gibb was one who was not placated by the second-hand McCartney quote. He continued throughout the morning of October 22 to place calls to the London office of Apple, but found the line to be constantly busy. It was obvious to Gibb that Apple had its hands full with calls from curious cluesters.

Gibb finally made a connection and found himself voice-to-voice with the Beatles' press agent Derek Taylor. Gibb began by asking Taylor about some of the clues and their meanings. "What about the 'turn me on, dead man' on 'Revolution 9'? Is that just a fluke?"

Taylor let out an audible sigh. "They're not that clever, you see. Most of that sort of thing is haphazard, and you see symbolism which is not in it. Most of those things are just done on the spur of the moment."

"Derek, these are questions that the kids are asking," Gibb said.

"Listen, don't worry about those questions. It's all coincidence. Paul McCartney isn't dead and the only proof we have that he's alive at this point is that he is." Taylor paused to let his last statement sink in. "You don't have to do any more than that to prove you're alive, except be alive. You don't have to produce yourself."

Maybe Derek Taylor didn't feel it was necessary for Paul to make a direct statement to WKNR or the rest of the media, but that's exactly what he did—just a short time after Russ Gibb's call to Apple.

At approximately 10:15 a.m., WKNR news director Philip Nye took a phone call from a man who said he was Paul McCartney. For the past ten days, many obvious hoaxers had called the station with the same story, but certain characteristics about this communication made Nye excited.

Russ Gibb was in the WKNR production room when Nye came bursting in. "Russ, I'm pretty sure I've got Paul on the line!"

Gibb looked up from the tape box he was scribbling upon. "You called him?"

"No, but it's definitely transatlantic and the guy on the phone knows things that only Paul could know. He remembers playing here in '64 and doing an interview with me before that show."

Gibb rose from the tape console. "We should record this."

After he and Nye made the necessary connections, Gibb reached for the phone receiver but then stopped in mid-grasp. He grinned and turned to the news director. "You better talk to him," Gibb said sheepishly, "he's probably pissed to the rungs at me."

Nye nodded and picked up the receiver. "Paul?"

A voice grunted affirmation.

"Paul, the kids here are saying you died in a car crash and have been replaced by a double. Further, it is believed that the Beatles have dropped hints to this on the record albums. What have you got to say about that?"

"Look," the voice on the other end began, "you originated this rumor with your initial broadcast. It was your station that created this sensationalism and all this rubbish...Russ Gibb started it all and I wish you would stop it."

"I told you he would be gunning for me," Gibb whispered.

Nye responded to McCartney's accusation. "No, we broadcasted what some fans had said."

"No," countered the indignant McCartney, "*you* started it and fed it with phone calls about me and letters about it. The rumor is a drag. People read things into the albums that just aren't there—things that are just accidents. We intended no symbolism whatsoever. But the Beatles can't control what people read into our music or our albums. There are a lot of songs stuck together to make fifty minutes of music. They don't mean anything."

"Okay," Nye nodded as if he and the musician were in the

same room. "Paul, we would like to play your comments on the air. Do we have your permission?"

"No, you can't."

"Can we say we talked to you?"

"Yes, but don't play the tape. If you do, other stations all over the country will call us and say they want the tape. Just because you created this sensation, why should you make anything more on it?"

"Come on," Nye pleaded, "just give us one statement to use over the air."

"No. If people want to hear my voice, let them listen to the new album. It was recorded last month. Tell them Paul McCartney is alive and moaning in London, England with his family."

"Paul, isn't there a way—"

"I've talked to you about thirty minutes," McCartney interrupted. "That's long enough. See you." There was a click and the phone went dead.

Nye placed the receiver back in its cradle. "He won't give us permission," he said to Gibb.

Gibb seemed undaunted. "Well, we can still use it. Remember that professor from Michigan State U. who called yesterday?"

Nye's face brightened. "Right! The guy who does voiceprints. He says that with the proper samples, he can identify the speaker. If we can prove that it was Paul who just called, we'll be getting somewhere."

Dr. Oscar Tosi of the MSU Department of Audiology and Speech was contacted and was soon supplied with a portion of the phone call and a segment of a WKNR interview from 1964. His method involved sending each audio sample through an oscilloscope (a device which creates visual representations of sound waves) and comparing the results. WKNR recorded Tosi's conclusion:

> TOSI: I would say that it would appear that this is the same man. However, I would like to have more samples to produce a really positive identification.

> WKNR: What makes you believe that this is the same

person?

> TOSI: We have a vowel, which is a very strong compo-
> nent, and we analyzed several performances and we found
> that the slopes, the width, the height are all the same, or at
> least look the same. And it's what makes us suppose that it
> is the same person. In general, when a person utters the
> same word, we have the same characteristics...or same
> point of similarity. When a different person utters the same
> word, we have differing characteristics. The Spectrogram
> will look, in general, the same, but the characteristics will
> be different, in the same way as two faces.

At the same time Tosi was delivering his findings, Dr. Henry M. Truby of the University of Miami conducted a similar experiment—but he concluded the opposite. Truby used samples from three Beatles songs sung by Paul McCartney ("Yesterday," "Penny Lane," and "Hey Jude") and produced three very different sonagrams. Does that mean there were *three* McCartneys? "I'm not prepared to say that this is the final word," Truby told *Rolling Stone* magazine, "but it's a beginning."

Ray Hoops, director of the Speech Sciences Laboratory at Wayne State University, scoffed at both men's findings. Voiceprints, he said, could chart a great many characteristics, but they cannot be used for identification. Nevertheless, Drs. Tosi and Truby found themselves taken seriously by newspapers throughout the country. Interview requests came fast and furious.

Although McCartney refused to give permission for the phone call to be aired on radio, verbatim transcripts of the conversation appeared the following day in several newspapers, including the *Detroit News* and the *Detroit Free Press*. Despite the fact that the phone call seemed to be legitimate, journalists began to wonder aloud the same question the cluesters had been asking: Why won't McCartney step forward into the light?

At 4:00 a.m. on October 23, the Dupont Circle park in Washington, D.C. was jammed with over seventy-five students from nearby George Washington University. "I Am the Walrus" wafted from the speakers of a portable tape player. Some students listened intently; others carried on dialogues as they sat on the edge of the fountain at the center of the park. As the song came to a frenzied end, a gaunt young man with a brown ponytail stood up and addressed the assemblage.

"That's Lennon's tribute to his dear departed friend, Paul." Mr. Ponytail scanned the crowd to be sure he had an audience. All those at his end of the park were at rapt attention, their faces bathed in the soft yellow glow of the street lamps. He continued: "Lennon tells us the story of what happened on the night McCartney was killed in a car crash. The song speaks of policemen standing in a row at the scene of the accident. There's a dead dog, who was probably hit when McCartney's car went out of control. They're waiting for a van to come; this van is an ambulance. Lennon says that he is crying, crying. No doubt he is shedding tears of grief. And, most important of all, he is the eggman."

Mr. Ponytail paused. Confused murmuring had started among members of the audience. "Don't you get it? An eggman delivers something—Lennon is delivering the sad news. And if that isn't easy for you to swallow, try this. The eggman in children's fairy tales is Humpty Dumpty. Anyone remember what happened to Humpty Dumpty?"

There were no answers from the crowd. "He cracked his head open in an accident—just like Paul," Mr. Ponytail informed the assembled cluesters. "And, as if all of this wasn't enough, Lennon included a death scene from Shakespere's *King Lear* at the end of the song. There are lines recited that point directly to Paul...lines like 'O, untimely death' and 'bury my body' and 'is he dead'." The young man bent down and pressed the rewind button on his tape machine. "Listen to the end again and you'll hear it."

Before the tape could be replayed, a voice called out from the crowd. "Do you think he's really dead?"

Mr. Ponytail flashed a toothy grin. "Well, that's for us to find out, isn't it?" He sat on the bench that had been serving as his headquarters for the past two hours. "The way I look at it, the truth has got to come out sometime soon. How long can a secret like this keep?"

"WGTB had a phone-in show today," another student interjected, "and they concluded that he's a dead man." Others in the group nodded; they'd heard the show, too. A pretty blond girl then stood up. She seemed a little shy as she tugged at her fingers. "Um, I think we should look at something that's not as obvious."

Mr. Ponytail motioned the girl toward the front. "Well, come on up and take the floor. Everyone's welcome to comment, especially lovely ladies." The girl gave a small embarrassed smile and stepped toward the bench. "Um, I've listened to Paul's instrument, the bass guitar, on all of the Beatles albums," she softly stated as she stroked the blond bangs from her eyes. "The style of Paul's playing has changed dramatically from 1964. If you listen to **A Hard Day's Night** and then to **Abbey Road**, you can hear the difference."

"Right!" agreed Mr. Ponytail. "She's got a good point. The bass is different on the Beatles' later albums. Is it really Paul McCartney's bass?"

"It's an imposter!" shouted most of the crowd in unison. Giggles then canvassed the park. Everyone was having a good time playing the macabre game. "Okay," Mr. Ponytail said as he raised his hands skyward, "now the event we've all been waiting for."

He stepped off of the bench and walked toward the phone booth across the street. There was no traffic at this hour, so the crowd moved en masse right behind him. When they got to the phone booth, they hushed down as Mr. Ponytail began feeding coins into the slot.

"The secret phone number holds the answer," Mr. Ponytail pronounced. "For those of you who are not hip to what I'm doing, I'll explain. There is a phone number hidden on the cover of **Magical Mystery Tour** and if you call the number, you will reach Billy Shears." He proceeded to dial and announced each digit as it was completed. "5...3...7...1...0...3...8...that's the secret number, gang."

The crowd of kids remained silent and waited for the result. After about a minute, Mr. Ponytail hung up and scooped his coins out of the change-return slot. He had a frown on his face as he emerged from the booth.

"You be the judge," he said. "I got a recording that told me the phone line was disconnected."

XV.
"One And One And One Is Three"
—"Come Together"
by the Beatles

Fred LaBour knocked softly on the door to the hotel room and fidgeted as he waited for a response. An attractive, conservatively-dressed woman opened the door and smiled as she extended her right hand in greeting.

"You must be Mr. LaBour," she deduced, motioning him inside. "Everybody else is here."

"Yeah, I'm sorry I'm late," he responded timidly as he followed the woman into the immense hotel suite. "I forgot to request a wake-up call."

Her sweet smile indicated that no harm had been done, but he remained nervous as he entered the lounge where half a dozen people sat. The conversation ceased and all eyes turned toward the new visitor.

"By the way, I'm Ginny," the attractive woman said, "and this is Allen Klein, the Beatles' new manager."

The disheveled overweight man on the couch nodded an emotionless acknowledgment toward LaBour.

Pointing to the men next to Klein, Ginny continued the introductions. "Paul Cannon from WKNR...and I believe you know Russ Gibb."

Gibb raised his hand in courteous regard. "Hi, kid. Glad to see you could make it."

As Fred managed a smile, Ginny motioned him through a doorway into a second lounge. Seated around a small wooden table were two more men. The well-dressed man, whom LaBour immediately recognized as F. Lee Bailey, quietly sipped a cup of coffee as he listened to the ravings of the other, who appeared to be commenting negatively on a newspaper article he was reading.

"What is this bullshit?" the red-haired man roared in a heavy British accent. "Who wrote this?"

As the man scanned the paper for a byline, Fred felt a sick feeling come over him as he realized that the article in question

73

was his own.

"Fred LaBour," the raging Englishman continued as he found the byline, "who is this person, Fred LaBour?"

Ginny's sweet smile disappeared, but she noticed that F. Lee Bailey was aware of their presence, so she announced the author's arrival. The British man turned out to be Paul's friend, musician Peter Asher. He scowled at LaBour and then left the room.

"Don't let him bother you," Bailey reassured, "he's just a hothead." The attorney ran his pencil down the legal pad before him. "Let's see...LaBour, LaBour...yes, you wrote about a great many of these clues."

Fred nodded as Bailey reached into a stack of record albums that were propped up against the air conditioning unit. He produced a copy of **Abbey Road** and laid it face-up on the table. Pointing to the license plate of the Volkswagen "Beetle" in the cover photo, he looked back up to LaBour.

"Now, what does this '28IF' mean?"

Fred looked to where Bailey's finger lay, cleared his throat, and explained the significance of the numbers and letters. "Uh, it means McCartney would be twenty-eight years old IF he had lived."

The attorney turned to his secretary. "Ginny, get the guy who owns this car on the phone."

As Ginny began dialing the London Motor Division, LaBour suddenly felt more at ease. Here was the famous attorney F. Lee Bailey playing the game on an even grander scale than he could ever imagine.

"So, Mr. LaBour, all of this is true?"

"Well, no," replied the student, "you see, I made it all up."

Bailey's expression became stern. He placed his pencil on the table and folded his hands across the legal pad. "Look, we have a one-hour TV show to do," he soberly stated, "so you're going to have to play along."

"Yeah, OK, I'll play along."

The attorney smiled and picked up the record album. "The show is going to be done like a courtroom trial. I'll ask you some questions pertaining to the clues and then I'll give you this album cover." Bailey handed the copy of **Abbey Road** to LaBour. "You'll pick up a Magic Marker and connect the dots on the reverse side to form the numeral '3', to indicate 3 Beatles. That's it. You got it?"

Fred nodded in agreement.

"Good," Bailey said. "We'll tape the show this afternoon."

* * * * * * * * *

"This is the RKO production of "Paul McCartney: The Complete Story, Told For The First and Last Time"...roll tape...and...cue talent."

On a set that resembled an authentic courtroom, F. Lee Bailey approached the occupied witness stand and rested his hand on its wooden frame. The harsh white glare of the television lights were playing upon the witness's eyeglasses, reflecting tiny orbs into the camera lens. "Will you tell us your name, please, sir?"

"Russ Gibb," the witness stated.

Calling your attention to the twelfth day of October of this year 1969, Mr. Gibbs [sic], in the afternoon, were you on duty and on the air?"

"Yes, sir."

"And did you receive a phone call from a listener about Paul McCartney, the Beatles' singer?"

"Yes, sir, I did."

"I draw your attention now to this reel of tape before me on the recorder," Bailey commanded, as he made an appropriated gesture toward a cumbersome grey Ampex two-track tape machine, "and I ask you if you can identify it."

Gibb craned his neck, more as a dramatic gesture than as an attempt to identify the tape; he already knew his next rehearsed line. "It looks like the tape that was taken off our log —we have to log all programming."

"Does it reproduce the conversation about McCartney?"

"Yes sir."

Bailey pushed the play button. As promised, the conversation between Russ Gibb and Tom issued from the clunky tape machine and filled the mock courtroom. The learned attorney paced slowly toward one of the cameras as he listened to the enigmatic dialogue. As the recording faded out, Bailey came upon a life-sized cardboard cutout of Paul McCartney and concentrated his gaze into the camera. "The witness, Mr. Gibb, has made a suggestion of death. The death of this man, Paul McCartney," Bailey indicated the cardboard effigy. "And others think that they may have some clues that Mr. McCartney is in fact dead, has been for some time and that his associates, the Beatles, are constantly trying to inform us of that fact.

"On the other hand, those who claim to be close to the Beatles say that there is nothing at all to it, that Paul is very much alive and nobody ever tried to suggest anything. We'll hear from those witnesses and hear what they have to say."

The camera zoomed into a tighter shot as Bailey continued his opening statement. "There is no judge in this case, because you are the judge. So hop into the chair, listen to the evidence, and decide whether Paul McCartney is dead and, if he is not dead, whether somebody is trying to persuade us that he is and, if so, for what reason."

After the sponsors assured the viewers that Tarreyton smokers would rather fight than switch and that Coca-Cola would like to teach the world to sing, court was back in session. Russ Gibb testified to the clues he had found in the songs, while Fred LaBour pointed out some of the more interesting visual clues on the **Abbey Road** cover. Paul Cannon, program director of WKNR, discussed the phone call the station received from a person who claimed to be Paul McCartney. This was followed by the testimony of a former employee of Apple who stated that the rumor infuriated the Beatles, because they couldn't get phone calls out through the jammed switchboards.

Paul's friend, Peter Asher, took the stand next and produced the show's most memorable exchange with F. Lee Bailey:

BAILEY: How do you explain the fact that on the cover of the Sgt. Pepper album, the only person of the many, many depicted who is shown with a hand held over his head is Paul McCartney?

ASHER: I think that's a coincidence. I mean, George Harrison is the only one with a large, bearded bald man above his head. I mean, it's just the way the picture came out.

BAILEY: Now, Mr. Asher, you claim that Paul is alive. That may well be so. You also claim that the Beatles did not deliberately try to create this myth in order to increase their publicity.

ASHER: That's what I know to be true, yes.

BAILEY: But it has increased their publicity hasn't it?

ASHER: Well, only because you people have taken it seriously enough to do all this incredible nonsense for an hour about something that really is just, you know, not true and in Paul's own words is bloody stupid.

BAILEY: *Life* magazine, too, is guilty of incredible nonsense, is it not?

ASHER: Yes, indeed...

BAILEY: And *Time* magazine is guilty of incredible nonsense?

ASHER: Well, you can't blame them anymore than one can blame you, because it's news. It's only news because people are stupid enough to want to believe it.

BAILEY: Do you think that it does any good at all for the Beatles to be thus publicized about a very fascinating possibility?

ASHER: I really don't know. I mean, I wouldn't be surprised if—you're probably right their record sales have probably increased because of this. But that's something that certainly doesn't concern them. They're not about to embark on some ridiculous publicity thing to try and sell more records. They've sold all the records that they'll ever need to sell.

BAILEY: You are, as you have put it, very close to him,

Paul McCartney.

ASHER: Yes, I am.

BAILEY: Well, isn't it a fact that even if you thought he was guilty of a little hoax here that you wouldn't say something?

ASHER: Oh, wow—so you mean that I'm lying to continue—

BAILEY: Oh, no, no, no. I'm saying that if you suspected that this might be going on I don't suggest that you're lying—but that you might be inclined to defend him in any event.

ASHER: Uh...that's probably true, yes, if I really thought that he was hoaxing, I'd probably back him up. But I swear to you that he is not, and that I know that he's alive and that he didn't mean for any of this to happen, nor did any of them.

BAILEY: So you say that you're not defending him because you don't have to, but if he were guilty of something, you probably would defend him anyway.

ASHER: I don't—no, no, no. That's a very unfair ending...

The Beatles' new manager Allen Klein was the last to appear on the witness stand. Klein must have felt a certain irony in his participation in the courtroom drama, for it was McCartney alone who balked at the decision by the other Beatles to install the crude but financially efficient New Yorker at the helm. He may have wished McCartney was out of the way, but he didn't display any feeling of that nature during his testimony, which was summed up by his final statement: "If what you and what some of the other media are suggesting is the truth, the Beatles would be harmed a great deal more. They don't have to stoop to this type of publicity in order to financially reward themselves."

Attorney Bailey took the floor for a brief closing statement. "Are people digging too hard to try to prove something that they only suspect? That's for you to judge. But we might say this: it is perfectly evident that if the Beatles wanted to, they could have—by this time—completely foreclosed this rumor. Such evidence has not been forthcoming from their end..." With that, the courtroom set went dark and one of the strangest shows ever produced for television was in the can.

The show eventually aired in syndication during the Thanksgiving weekend (November 27-30, 1969) on WOR in New York and also in the Boston, San Francisco, and Los Angeles markets. After this single broadcast, the videotape of the program vanished. It remains to this day one of the most sought-after, but hopelessly-lost, pieces of Beatles history.

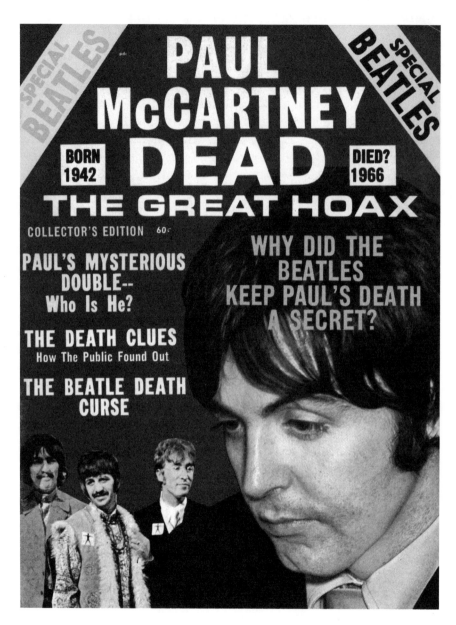

PAUL McCARTNEY DEAD—THE GREAT HOAX MAGAZINE
An entire magazine devoted to the macabre story. It was a bestseller.
(Photo from the author's collection.)

XVI.
"I Know What It's Like To Be Dead"
—"She Said, She Said"
by the Beatles

A virtual enterprise developed overnight, as the macabre stories about Paul McCartney inspired the production of saleable merchandise. Scores of ghoulish entrepreneurs saw the possibilities for big money and jumped onto the McCartney "death" wagon. RKO Film and Television, as we have seen, hopped on first with the F. Lee Bailey courtroom drama. There were, however, many other examples of Good Old American Capitalism already in motion.

In New York City, Country Wide Publications created an entire magazine based on the rumor. *Paul McCartney Dead—The Great Hoax* was filled with sixty-six pages of sensationally-titled articles that ran the gamut from "The Beatle Death Curse" to "Paul's Wedding: Who Did Linda Eastman Really Marry?" The first press run sold out quickly.

Although aimed primarily at the teeny-bopper audience, some of the articles in the magazine tended toward mature discussions of metaphysics and theology. An example is a piece called "Do The Beatles Really Mourn Paul's Death?":

> What is the meaning of reality and existence? Is there actually such a thing as death? Or are we all just a part of a cosmic whole? These are questions which the Beatles have asked continually since the ill-fated winter of 1966. Can the memory of a devoted friend be easily erased if you still feel that friend is near you, that part of him is a part of you? The answer for the Beatles was "No!"
>
> If not in body, Paul's soul is alive. He lives in the bodies of John Lennon, George Harrison, Ringo Starr, and one more. That fourth person looks like Paul and even has some of the same mannerisms as Paul. And whether or not he was born Paul McCartney is irrelevant. Even if the real Paul McCartney lies somewhere in a tiny churchyard, he can never die. For when you believe hard enough, anything is possible!

81

And resurrection was the theme in "Paul Died And Was Reborn—An Explanation For Those Who Are Believers":

> Of course, the belief in death and rebirth is not confined to the Hindu sects or the users of drugs. In a deeply spiritual sense, the Christian religion speaks of being reborn, of becoming a new person. Over and over again, in the New Testament, there is talk of being born again, of becoming a new person, in a spiritual sense. There is the familiar and inspiring story of Lazarus, raised from the tomb, and the account of the resurrection of Christ.
>
> Isn't it possible that the Beatles believe, in a spiritual sense, that Paul does live on, through his music, and through those who knew, respected and loved him?
>
> It could well be that the Beatles, moved by this universal desire to ensure the immortality of their friend, Paul, truly believe that, in a mystical sense, he is alive. There is no hoax here, in the usual sense of the word, no desire to fool an unsuspecting public. Rather, there is a need to prove the immortality of one member of their group.
>
> If listeners have enough spiritual awareness to believe, as the Beatles do, in the immortality of the human spirit, they will pick up [the hidden] clues and be reassured that in a very real sense, Paul does survive. And for those who lack this degree of spiritual development, the deeper truth will still be concealed.

The editors of *Paul McCartney Dead—The Great Hoax* concluded that the real Paul was dead and the remaining Beatles covered up the truth. "We rejoice with the Beatles," the final line in the publication stated, "for it means that they have truly succeeded in their incredible hoax." Priced at an economical sixty cents, information-hungry cluesters flocked to the newsstands and bought up all the available copies, forcing Country Wide to cheerfully restart the presses for a second printing.

Novelty records have always been a successful method by which to cash in on a fad. The MGM label backed a band called The Mystery Tour, whose morbid offering—"The Ballad of Paul"—became the first and most successful of this genre. The song was basically a rhyming recitation of death clues that the singer claimed to have discovered on Beatles records.

Clues to the strangest puzzle of our time.

The
Ballad
Of

K-14097

The Mystery Tour
A provocative new single from

MGM
RECORDS

MGM Records is a division of Metro-Goldwyn-Mayer Inc.

FULL-PAGE ADVERTISEMENT
for the "Ballad of Paul" novelty single, one of two ads (see page 86) to
appear in *Billboard* magazine to hawk "Paul-is-Dead" singles
that were released in the rumor's wake.
(Photo courtesy Cascargo Music/Brent Gordon.)

Has Paul McCartney left this world?
Has he taken his last breath?
Have John and George and Ringo
Told us of his death?

It never made the papers
You didn't read it in the news
But it's all right there for you to find
In several hidden clues.

From Sgt. Pepper to Abbey Road,
They led us on a chase
And if you know just where to look,
It all falls into place.

An argument, an accident
An unseen traffic light
A left-hand guitar on a fresh-dug grave.

An album done in mourning white
And a Magical Mystery Tour
Three inside with blood-red rose
One death-black makes four.

Song lyrics are important
In fact, they say it all
At the end of "Strawberry Fields,"
John says, "I buried Paul."

Four men on the front of Abbey Road
Cross a London street
The first in white, the next in black
The third with no shoes on his feet.

A cigarette is dangling
From the right hand of the dead
McCartney was left-handed
So everyone has said.

These are just a few things
That I have found
Is he somewhere on that British Isle,
Buried in the ground?

84

An outfit calling itself Zacherias & The Tree People also appeared on the record shelves with their satirically-titled novelty, "We're All Paulbearers."

Even though he wear no shoes,
It sure looks like him
There were four in Liverpool
Now there's only three of them.

We're all Paulbearers
You and I

See the crash insinuation
O.P.D. on his sleeve
Wearing black sweet carnation
While three play Misery.

If it's a hoax,
We're none the wiser
Why make the people cry?
We're all Paulbearers
You and I.

Copyright 1969 Don Tweedy Music,
ASCAP Copyright control

WTIX radio in New Orleans commissioned a theme song for their coverage of the rumor. A group called Billy Shears & The All-Americans came up with the threnody "Brother Paul." Public demand for copies of the song encouraged its official release one week later on Shelby Singleton's Silver Fox Records label.

Brother Paul, I'm crying
Are you really lying
Every night and day
Beneath the cold and lonely stone?

Are you getting older
Or just getting colder?
Brother Paul, where did you fall
And are you still alone?

FULL-PAGE ADVERTISEMENT
for the "Brother Paul" novelty single, one of two ads (see page 83) to
appear in *Billboard* magazine to hawk "Paul-is-Dead" singles
that were released in the rumor's wake.
(Photo courtesy Shelby Singleton Music.)

Can You hear me singing, Brother Paul?
Can you stand and sing your song?
Did you hear the trumpet when it called?
Can you tell me, is it true
Are you gone?

Brother Paul, you're missing
If you can, please listen
Give me a sign to hope
That you are still around.

Are you just a dancer?
Tell me, can you answer?
Can your words be heard
As only echoes from the ground?

Should we light a candle, Brother Paul?
Could you see the flame that shone?
Should the bells be ringing, Brother Paul?
Could you find your way?
Are you gone?

Over at RCA Records, José Feliciano (the blind flamenco guitarist whose greatest claim to fame came five years later with the self-penned theme song to the TV series "Chico and the Man"), contributed his entry. Although it was announced to *Billboard* magazine that the song was to come out under his own name, Feliciano apparently had a last-minute change of heart because "So Long, Paul" was released under the curious pseudonym Werbley Finster.

I heard the radio the other day
I heard something that blew my mind
It was something that I didn't
Even believe at all

The news concerned itself
With a young man everybody knows
And they said that he went running
Taking off his clothes

All the girls are crying
'Cause they think that Paul is gone
I was over in England
And I know that that's not so

They may tell you
Anything that they want
But let me tell you, darlin'
Everything's gonna be all right, yeah

Well, I know and I believe
That it's all right
'Cause I think Paul
Had himself a Hard Day's Night

I tell ya, I'm gonna
Preach it all over the land
'Cause I can tell you now
That Paul's gonna hold your hand

So Long, Paul
We hate to see you go
So Long, Paul
After making all that dough

This cluster of novelty singles hit the record racks during the last week of November—too late to take advantage of the rapidly-fading craze. Except for "The Ballad of Paul," all failed to chart on the *Billboard* Hot 100 Singles list and they sank without a trace.

Aside from the novelty songs and the "Paul-is-Dead" magazine, the other attempted cash-in happened, not in the United States, but in Canada. There were some old tracks (circa 1961) by a British musician named Tony Sheridan that featured the Beatles as the backing band. These recordings, although of great historic value, never became a formidable commercial success. In November of 1969, Polydor Records of Canada decided what they needed was an eye-catching cover to move the merchandise. The rumor provided the inspiration.

VERY TOGETHER ALBUM JACKET
Canadian Polydor's cash-in on the controversy alluded to the rumor on a
repackaging of the Tony Sheridan tapes. Was Paul McCartney "snuffed out"?
(Photo from the author's collection.)

The collection, entitled **Very Together** (Polydor Special 242.008), featured a jacket photograph by Jean-Patrick Amish. It depicted a candelabra with four holders—the second candle just having been extinguished. The reference must have been missed by the record-buying public, because this incarnation of the Sheridan/Beatles sessions didn't sell either.

At the Tower Records shop in Los Angeles, dozens of kids stood in the line at the register. Clutched in their hands were the last copies of the "clue albums," as the clerks had begun to refer to them. Over the in-house stereo system, Joe Cocker's new single, "Delta Lady" was playing, but no one seemed to be listening. The West Coast cluesters were instead absorbed in the artwork of the records they were about to purchase. But when Cocker's plaintive growl faded and the next single dropped onto the turntable, the atmosphere became charged with community energy.

"Here come ol' flattop," sang John Lennon as "Come To-gether" throbbed through the speakers. The kids looked at each other as knowing grins filled their faces. They began to sing along with the song, quietly at first, until the stanza that commenced with the line "One and one and one is three. " With that, the cluesters jabbed fingers in the air to emphasize each number and shouted a parody of the lyrics:

ONE AND ONE AND ONE IS THREE!!!
JOHN AND GEORGE AND RINGO...
BUT PAUL IS HISTORY!!!

The scene was similar throughout the country. An enter-prising manager in the Midwest decided to simplify matters at his record store. He took the four "clue albums," created an attractive black box for them, and offered the result as a "Paul McCartney Funeral Pack." Another retailer published a "Clue Guide" which he gave out free with the purchase of any Beatles album.

Record stores across the country were having a difficult time keeping **Sgt. Pepper, Magical Mystery Tour,** the "White Album" and **Abbey Road** in stock. The situation had gotten so urgent that the distributors, on their daily deliveries, would always leave a box of each album with the retail outlets without even consulting the order forms.

Variety duly noted the explosion of sales in a November 5 article. "Rumors of Paul McCartney's death have not hurt sales of the Beatles' most recent LP, **Abbey Road,**" the magazine reported. "On the contrary, the ballyhoo seems to have spurted sales into an all-time peak pace for the British combo. The album, out about four weeks, has racked up sales of over 2,500,000 disk copies while the cartridge and cassette sales are now around 400,000 units."

Capitol Records kept their plants operating overtime to meet the demand. It was not surprising that the record label did nothing to discourage the rumor. Along with **Abbey Road**, the Beatles' back catalogue was selling out of the box. The "death" of Paul McCartney had given the old albums a new lease on life, and Capitol couldn't be happier to help with the funeral.

XVII.
"With Lovers And Friends, I Still Can Recall Some Are Dead And Some Are Living"
—"In My Life"
by the Beatles

Drake University's *Times-Delphic* was the first college newspaper to publish an article about the McCartney rumor with "Is Beatle Paul McCartney Dead?" on September 17, 1969. The author, Tim Harper, has been largely forgotten for his part in the drama as the years have ticked by, but in October of 1969, he was heavily in demand for paid interviews.

The *Chicago Sun-Times* disclosed in its October 21 issue that Harper, not Russ Gibb or Fred LaBour, had been the first to officially publicize the possibility of McCartney's death. This immediately led to a barrage of phone calls to Harper from radio and TV stations eager for interviews. Mike Lee, a correspondent for ABC in Iowa, contacted Harper and offered to act as his agent. Harper agreed, and Lee promptly secured $150 worth of interviews with stations such as WDGY (Minneapolis), KIMN (Denver), KQV (Pittsburgh), KGBS (Los Angeles), KLEO (Wichita), and WIND (Chicago). "I don't know how far this thing will go," Lee told the *Drake Times-Delphic*, "but I'm still getting calls from radio stations."

The producer of Ronnie Barrett's talk show "Chicago" was so intent on getting Harper to the WLS television studio on time that he authorized the charter of a private plane at a cost of $192. "That boy and his Beatle story are news," explained Merrill Mazner to the *Des Moines Register*. "It was worth every penny for the cost of the trip."

In terms of media coverage, the rumor reached an apex during the last two weeks of October. Major newspapers and network television had avoided comment up to this point, for they assumed that, like the rumors of the past, the story would fade before the presses had a chance to warm up. However, by October 21, it became apparent that the innuendo surrounding the Beatles would not die. The fact that the rumor-mongering and clue-hunting had become a bona fide sociological phenomenon prompted many news editors to devote several column-inches to the story.

From coast to coast the rumor garnered coverage in newspapers no less respected than *The New York Times*, *The Washington Post* and *The Chicago Tribune*. The *Times*, in fact, even went to the trouble of enlisting rock journalist J Marks to pen their article, primarily because of his working relationship with the former Linda Eastman (they had collaborated in 1967 on a book-and-record project entitled *Rock And Other Four-Letter Words*).

While the media in America filled the pages and airwaves with commentary, the British journalists generally kept the rumor at arm's length. Even the Fleet Street tabloids, notorious for their sensationalistic headlines, scarcely made mention of the mystery. The usually staid *London Evening Standard* was the only newspaper to offer anything substantive. Ray Connolly, a man with apparent Beatle connections, wrote: "Despite everything you may have heard in the last few days, Beatle Paul McCartney is alive and well. I have this on very good authority —he told me himself."* McCartney was quoted as saying, "I'm dead am I? Why does nobody ever tell me anything?" The article had a primarily sardonic tone to it as it mocked the foolishness of American fans who put credence in the rumor.

Despite the *Evening Standard*'s denunciation and the lack of media saturation in general, hundreds of British teenagers caught wind of the story anyway and they set up a vigil outside of Paul's home in St. Johns Wood.

The Beatle and his new family were indeed inside, but this recent invasion of their privacy set the gears in motion for a quick evacuation. Paul placed a call to Derek Taylor and informed him that the McCartney clan was leaving England for a holiday retreat in Scotland. Paul had recently purchased an old farmhouse in a secluded spot near Campbelltown and it would be the perfect place to escape all of the craziness.

---

*"I Didn't Know I was Dead—Beatle Paul," by Ray Connolly; *London Evening Standard* (October 22, 1969).

92

While on the phone, Taylor once again attempted to coax McCartney toward making a personal appearance in order to quash the rumor. The calls to Apple had mounted to over a thousand per day, and this was severely hindering the normal operation of the Beatles' entertainment empire. Paul seemed unconcerned and again refused to meet with any press representatives. He and Linda (and Heather and little Mary) were going to pack their bags and try to have a holiday like a normal family. That was that.

Television news got into the act. Local stations reported on the rumor and featured interviews with their regional "clue experts." Not to be outdone, the networks followed the continuing saga and revealed the latest details for the better part of the week. ABC, in particular, devoted more air time to the rumor than to President Nixon. It all culminated with a 2:02 taped report on the October 23 newscast.

"The British government is about to launch a nationwide crackdown on drug pushers," ABC anchor Howard K. Smith told his viewers. "Queen Elizabeth is expected to announce the action herself in a speech before Parliament next Tuesday..."

The picture on the screen behind Smith dissolved from a British flag into a photograph of Paul McCartney on a field of question marks. "There's little likelihood that she will say anything about a big mystery surrounding one of her most famous subjects, Beatle Paul McCartney. A rumor that he is dead has been stoutly denied by several people, including Paul. There is even one report that McCartney was killed three years ago in an auto accident and a double put in his place. For a report on how it all got started, here is ABC's Gregory Jackson..."

The scene cut to the young reporter seated behind a phonograph turntable. "As any parent can testify," Jackson began, "the lifestyle of the Beatles has always been somewhat different. And if you believe current rumor, their style of revealing Paul McCartney's alleged death has been carried out with singular taste."

Jackson related several of the clues and used visual aids

93

to emphasize the implication. He then turned to the phonograph and placed the tone arm onto a record album. "Some of the clues are said to be found by playing the records at different speeds or even backwards. And there is a degree of truth to it. For example, in the song 'I Am the Walrus,' we play it here on this record and tape the play and then run the tape backwards. And if you listen closely, you can hear someone saying, over and over, 'Paul is dead'..."

The camera zoomed in on the spinning disc as the audio issued forth: "Ha ha, Paul is dead...ha ha, Paul is dead...ha ha, Paul is dead..." The camera panned back to Jackson.

"In London, Paul McCartney has been vehemently denying his death. Here in New York, the city's largest record store said today that the Beatles' latest album [**Abbey Road**] cost about two dollars more than the past albums and...they haven't been selling very well. At least up to now, before the rumor started."

NBC may not have given the same amount of air time to the controversy as ABC, but many viewers were shocked when John Chancellor summed up the entire event with this statement: "All we can report with certainty is that Paul McCartney is either dead or alive."

Unbeknownst to Chancellor or any of the other news anchors, on that very evening, an AP staff photographer obtained the first visual evidence of McCartney's existence since the onset of the rumor. Staked out at Glasgow Airport, the photographer spotted the McCartney family as they entered the terminal after disembarking a shuttle flight. He snapped a quick succession of shots as the family hurried to a waiting car. By 8:00 p.m. E.S.T., a photo was on the wires.

The next night on ABC, Frank Reynolds showed the photo. "Well, there he is. He walks, he talks, he sings—Paul McCartney of the Beatles. He finally got in front of a camera in Glasgow to put an end to the speculation that he is no longer among the living. He *is*—and now the whole world has been apprised of that fact."

The other networks and many newspapers showed the photograph as well. But did that put an end to the rumor? Don't

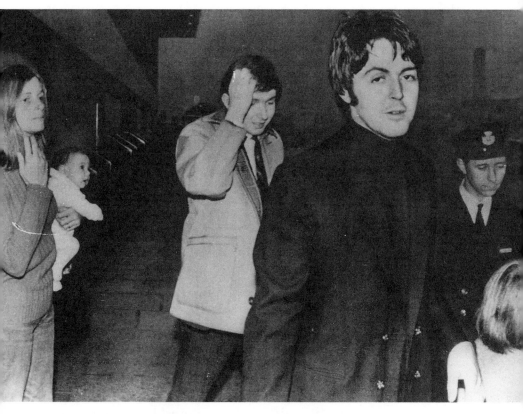

PAUL MCCARTNEY AND FAMILY IN GLASGOW
The first visual evidence of Paul McCartney's existence since the rumor began.
This photo was taken on October 23 as the McCartney family arrived
at Glasgow Airport en route to Paul's Campbelltown farm.
(Photo courtesy AP/Wide World Photos.)

bet your life on it...

Despite the Glasgow Airport photo, worried fans and curious media continued to inundate the Apple offices with inquiries about McCartney. At this point, *Life* magazine decided to end the speculation about the musician's well-being once and for all. Dorothy Bacon, the magazine's London correspondent, was dispatched to the McCartney's farmhouse in High Park, Campbelltown, Scotland. Accompanying Bacon were two staff photographers who were instructed to bring back any visual evidence of Paul's existence, even if he refused to be interviewed.

The team of journalists trekked through the marshy Scottish countryside on foot, their cameras and notepads at the ready. Once they spotted the modest ramshackle farmhouse, they quickened their pace and excitedly chatted among one another. The sound of their voices brought Martha, Paul's huge sheepdog, barreling down the hill to greet them and her barking in turn brought Paul running.

"What is this?" McCartney demanded as he came face to face with the troop. "You bastards are trespassing on my property! Get out of here!"

The sight of an angry, unshaven Paul McCartney brought the cameras out of their holsters. The photographers took a dozen pictures of the raving Beatle ordering them to get the hell off his land. As Bacon attempted to ask McCartney some questions, the musician grabbed a bucket of water and heaved it onto the nearest cameraman. More shutters clicked, but the *Life* team realized that they had overstayed their welcome. They headed back down the hill, a still-fuming McCartney eyeing their retreat across the boglands.

Within minutes of their departure, the journalists found themselves once again in the presence of Paul McCartney. Having realized the consequences of what he had done, the musician had hopped into his Land-Rover jeep and chased down the reporter.

"Look, I'm sorry for that temper tantrum of mine," McCartney apologized, "but I'm just tired of my privacy being infringed upon."

THE CASE OF THE 'MISSING' BEATLE

Paul is still with us

Paul and
his family
last week
in Scotland

NOVEMBER 7 · 1969 · 40¢

McCARTNEY ON THE COVER OF *LIFE* MAGAZINE
Paul reportedly heaved a bucket of water at *Life* magazine photographers
when they trespassed on his property in Scotland. He later apologized
and ended up as the cover story of the November 7 issue.

(Photo courtesy Time/Life, Inc.)

"We're just trying to do our jobs, Mr. McCartney," Bacon responded. "Now that you're here, will you give us an interview, then?"

McCartney smiled. "Of course, my dear—in return for that film you just shot. You got my bad side anyway."

The musician was a completely different person than he had been only moments before. He escorted the troop back to his farmhouse and served everyone tea. Linda came outside and stood beside her husband, newborn Mary in her arms. New photographs were taken of the happy family, while Paul delivered a statement for the readers of *Life*.

"It is all bloody stupid," he was quoted in part, "perhaps the rumor started because I haven't been much in the press lately. I have done enough press for a lifetime and I don't have anything to say these days...can you spread it around that I am just an ordinary person and want to live in peace?"*

Paul McCartney had managed once again to charm the press. The temper tantrum photos were never used.

---

*Perhaps overshadowed by the rumor controversy, a very intriguing statement by McCartney to *Life* was passed over by press and fans alike. It indicated the Beatles were on the verge of breaking up: "...the Beatle thing is over. It has been exploded, partly by what we have done and partly by other people."

XVIII.
"Open Up Your Eyes Now
Tell Me What You See"
—"Tell Me What You See"
by the Beatles

"This is WNEW in New York...in a moment, Christopher Glenn takes a look at the rumor that has grabbed the attention of the country, if not the world...is Paul McCartney dead?..."

"Colby, you dog!" George Stone slapped his roommate on the back. "This is a chance for you to let me win back my twenty bucks. I say McCartney's alive."

Colby Andersson and George Stone were students at New York University. Just three weeks before, the only thing on their minds was the 1969 World Series, a tournament which pitted the heavily-favored Baltimore Orioles against the Mets. A Brooklynese by birth, Colby naturally supported his home team and accepted a wager offered by his skeptical dorm buddy. The Amazing Mets took the Series in five games and George found himself twenty dollars poorer.

On this Saturday afternoon during the last week of October, the Mets were still heroes at NYU. However, the victory was now only a sweet memory and the students were focused instead on the story of the year.

"I'm not betting you," Colby said as he defiantly dragged on a Marlboro. "Besides, how can you prove it?"

"I'll show you after the radio program," George promised.

The two turned their attention to a small General Electric radio. The signal was weak, so Colby rose from his seat and adjusted the coat hanger that served as the radio's antennae. The reception didn't get much better until George smacked the side of the unit with his open palm. "It's all in the wrist," George said triumphantly.

"This is Christopher Glenn," the documentary began. "I personally do not believe the raging rumors about Paul McCartney, but that doesn't mean you can't, if you want to. At the outset, let's divulge that the man who is generally credited with providing the first compendium of clues about Paul's death doesn't

99

believe he's dead. He's John Summer, a junior at Ohio Wesleyan University..."

"That's bull," Colby assured his roommate, "I heard that a deejay in Detroit started it."

"Well, I listened to some guy named Lew Yager from Hofstra University on WABC and he said he started it," George countered.

The voice of John Summer brought the two men back to the radio. "I don't believe that Paul is dead, but I believe this was intentional, that they wanted the masses to discover these inferences to Paul's death and take it as such and then let the rumor pass over."

"Why would they want to do this?" asked Glenn.

"For their own enjoyment," Summer continued. "It can't be anything else, really. It can't be publicity, because they certainly don't need it. How far can you go in the musical field without getting a bit bored? Maybe they'd like to test something on the public, you know, test reaction. I imagine they probably get a big kick out of it. I don't think they expected it to go this far, really..."

Colby turned down the radio's volume. "That's what I think. The Beatles are playing a game with us."

"That could be, but I can still prove he's alive. " George thrust his hand outward. "Bet me."

Colby engaged in the handshake. "Okay, pal—prove it!"

Without rising from his chair near the radio, George reached over to his desk. He retrieved an oversized magazine and tossed it on his friend's lap. "I got it in the mail today. Pay up."

Colby stared at the magazine's cover. It was *Life*'s latest issue and it featured the banner headline, "Paul Is Still With Us: The Case of the 'Missing' Beatle." With the Scottish landscape serving as a backdrop, the entire McCartney clan stood in a classic family pose. Inside, a four-page article by John Neary outlined the phenomenon and it was capped-off by McCartney's wearied plea that he be left alone.

"Yeah, someone in my English lit class showed this to me yesterday," Colby finally said, "but let *me* show *you* something." Colby opened the cover page of the magazine. He held it up to a small lamp next to the radio, in order to back-light the photo of McCartney. There was an advertisement for a Lincoln Continental automobile on the reverse of the cover page. The bright light made the page translucent, allowing the photographs on both sides to be superimposed.

"Pretty eerie, huh?" Colby asked.

George was silent. In fact, he was freaked at what he saw.

It appeared that the automobile had impaled the body of Paul McCartney.

XIX.
"Hey, It's Just Insanity,
But It's A Great Plug For Abbey Road."
—John Lennon,
October 24 phone interview with WKNR

By Friday, October 24, Paul's unintentional but crucial appearance in the Glasgow Airport photo had put many young people's minds at ease. Those who received advance copies of *Life* magazine were also treated to a visual confirmation of the elusive Beatle. These photos proved that the rumor was false, didn't they? Well, sort of...

Despite the mounting evidence that Paul was alive, the game continued. "Paul-is-Dead" cognoscenti began to take the rumor to different levels. One faction still maintained that McCartney had perished in 1966 and had been replaced by a double. It was this "double" who appeared in the Glasgow and *Life* photos and, indeed, all photos since 1966. It was this imposter "Paul" who sang on "Hey Jude" and "Lady Madonna"; the voice on those songs didn't sound very much like the voice that sang on "Yesterday."

While the Look-a-Like Faction continued to search for clues, a new sect began to emerge around this time. This group, informally known as the Beatle Hoax Faction, believed that the clues were placed on the albums to promote sales. "I'm pretty sure he is alive," John Summer told the *Ohio State Lantern*, [but] I don't take much stock in the fact that the rumor has been disclaimed."

Summer and other campus sleuths were of the opinion that Paul McCartney was being "singled out" on album covers and in song lyrics. The degree of truth in this observation kept the fires of the rumor burning. It was a fact, pointed out the cluesters, that Paul was the only Beatle with his back turned toward the camera on the cover of **Sgt. Pepper's**. Paul was barefoot and out of step on the cover of **Abbey Road**. And who was the Walrus? "The walrus was Paul," according to John Lennon when he sang that line in the song, "Glass Onion."

These and dozens of other references to Paul were purposely placed on the albums to cause fans to notice a pattern. The Beatles were hoping the public would discover these clues, spread the rumor to their friends and purchase more albums in order to search for further evidence, concluded the Beatle Hoax Faction.

It wasn't just the college kids who put credence in this theory. "It's the most well-planned publicity stunt ever," WAKR deejay Tony Jay told the *Akron Beacon Journal*. "Only the Beatles could do it...so subtly with the planting of symbols of death. Because of the sophisticated young people today, [the Beatles] knew their clues would eventually be discovered."

One undeniable fact became apparent; sales of Beatles albums *did* increase. **Abbey Road** rocketed to number one and the three other albums germane to the rumor (**Sgt. Pepper's, Magical Mystery Tour**, and the "White Album") resurfaced on the *Billboard* Top 200 LP chart after absences of up to a year-and-a-half. Rocco Catena, Capitol Records Vice-President of National Merchandising, found this development to his liking. "From the looks of it, this is going to be the biggest month in history in terms of Beatles sales," he proudly proclaimed to *Rolling Stone* magazine.

But would the Beatles really need to create a hoax for financial reward? By 1966, the band was certainly one of the most popular and monetarily successful musical acts in history. John, Paul, George, and Ringo had become millionaires many times over and had seriously challenged Elvis Presley for the honor of The Greatest Rock 'n' Roll Act. It is therefore highly unlikely that, if a Beatles-generated hoax had been concocted, it was for the money.

While many of the sleuths may have agreed with this supposition, they nonetheless indicated that Capitol Records may have chosen to perpetrate the "Paul-is-Dead" rumor for *their* financial benefit. "I always thought that if I owned a record label, I would have done something like that," says Michael LaBricque, a former Michigan student. "A lot of my friends and myself saw the dollar signs when everyone was following the rumor."

LaBricque was among the many college students who

went on clue hunts. "I realized it was all a game—a scavenger hunt—but I was and I am sure to this day that it was set up by the record company. But *even* if they didn't start it, they certainly didn't do anything to stop it."

Behind every great artist, there is someone running the cash register. In the case of the Beatles, the U.S. record label Capitol traded plastic discs to the public for money. While this is the name of the game in the music industry, some of Capitol's business practices in this regard were decidedly carnivorous.

Unlike the Parlophone/EMI releases in Great Britain (and "The Rest of The World") that offered the record-buyer a fourteen-track unexpunged product, Capitol's versions for U.S. consumption were usually truncated to ten cuts. This was done so that after two or three albums, Capitol could offer U.S. fans a "new" Beatles album, built from the excised British songs. The Beatles found Capitol's money-grubbing tactics tasteless and unfair to their loyal American audience, but little comment was made until the infamous "Butcher" controversy.

In 1966, Capitol assembled an album from their "archives," taking the four songs chopped from the British edition of **Rubber Soul**, three from the soon-to-be-released **Revolver**, and four non-LP singles. The collection, to be titled **Yesterday...and Today,** needed a Fab Four photograph for the cover, so the Beatles got together for a photo session and sent the outcome off to the States.

Since the album was a result of Capitol's "butchering" of the British releases, the group found their concept for the cover to be cleverly appropriate. It featured the Beatles attired in meat-cutter's smocks, with decapitated baby dolls clutched in their hands and raw meat strewn across their laps. Somehow, this cover actually made it onto the market for one day, before being hastily recalled. A less-offensive cover was substituted, but the Beatles must have made their point. After the **Revolver** album, all Capitol releases bore the same unaltered configuration as the British counterparts.

The Beatles weren't the only music act affected by Capitol's insatiable appetite for product. The Beach Boys felt the heat generated by the corporate honchos and often produced *three* albums of material per year during their early career. Capitol's constant demand for new albums led to the issuance of mediocre collections with five or six fine songs and a lot of uninspired filler.

And, if that wasn't bad enough, Capitol took Brian Wilson's pristine monophonic productions and manufactured artificial stereo versions of the albums. The process, dubbed *duophonic stereo*, consisted of adding a millisecond of echo to one channel of the recording. This did not create stereo; it only served to muddy-up the music.

Capitol's history of greed notwithstanding, they denied that they inaugurated any sort of a death hoax in order to move merchandise. It is most likely they were telling the truth ("There are no press agents so imaginative," *Variety* magazine sarcastically noted). It would be virtually impossible to engineer a publicity stunt on such a grand scale and then successfully cover up the footprints; surely, someone would have talked about it or written an expose about the part the label played in the Greatest Advertising Concept in History. This has not happened in the two decades since the rumor swept the world.

It is probably true, as former student LaBricque suggested, that the label *did* keep its corporate mouth shut, so as not to disturb the golden goose that began to lay *aurum ova* on their laps.

XX.
"Don't Be Surprised If You Hear
Rumors That I Am Dead."
—Paul McCartney, in a phone call to his father,
as quoted in the *Liverpool Daily Post* (Oct. 22, 1969)

On Sunday, October 26, thousands of radios in Detroit were tuned to WKNR for "The Beatles Plot." This was the show Russ Gibb, Dan Carlisle, and John Small had been working on for the better part of the last week, and heavy promotion had delivered a large audience.

The scope of research for the radio program was nothing less than extensive. Not only had the station devoted scores of man-hours toward the uncovering of clues; money was also spent to send Gibb on a pilgrimage to the Apple offices in London. "I hung around Apple for two or three days," Gibb recently related. "They thought I was a total jerk. And they weren't any help at all."

Although he was unable to locate the missing McCartney, Russ did contact Eric Clapton while overseas. As well as having played with Blind Faith at Gibb's Grande Ballroom, Clapton had recently performed with John Lennon in Toronto and contributed lead guitar to the Beatles' "White Album." "I must admit, I'm as convinced as anybody could be [about the coincidences]," he told Gibb.

"You haven't seen him in six months, right?"

"I've seen photographs," Clapton replied, "and he looked as though he put on a little weight..."

During the show, the three deejays took turns revealing the audio and visual clues, all the time building up their case that something mysterious was going on. "Now, are all of these things coincidences?" Small asked rhetorically. "Are we being duped into believing all of this? Apple Records seems to want us to believe this. But we don't."

Those who listened to WKNR that Sunday evening were taken through a whirlwind of speculation. Was the 'O.P.D.' on Paul's shoulder an acronym for 'Officially Pronounced Dead'? Did John Lennon utter "I buried Paul" at the end of "Strawberry

Fields Forever"? Was there a secret dialogue of death contained within "Revolution 9"? Gibb, Carlisle and Small gave the impression that the clues did exist and they brought in all sorts of people who claimed that they hadn't seen McCartney anywhere for months.

John Lennon also appeared on the WKNR program, via a telephone interview with John Small:

> SMALL: What have you got to say about the backward movement of some of these records?

> LENNON: Sure, you can play anything backwards and you're going to get different connotations. I don't know what Beatles records sound like backwards—I never play them backwards.

> SMALL: Well, what about the **Abbey Road** thing, John, where the bare feet of Paul McCartney would sort of indicate death to some.

> LENNON: Paul walks barefoot across the road because Paul's idea of being different is to look almost straight but just have his ear painted blue, you know—something a little subtle. That's his little gimmick, that's all.

> SMALL: How has this affected you mentally?

> LENNON: It's the most stupid rumor I've ever heard.

Despite Lennon's denial that the Beatles were playing a devious joke upon the public, the thrust of the WKNR program indeed pointed to a Beatles-engineered hoax. After an hour-and-a-half of clue discussion and interviews, Russ Gibb delivered a sober commentary to close the show:

> I think Paul McCartney is alive. And I think that the Beatles have gotten themselves involved in a charlatan game. I feel that they have been hot and cold on this game. And that what started out as a rebuttal to John's comment about the Beatles being more popular than Jesus Christ started John into thinking and he rapped this out with the other fellows and they have proceeded to play the game.

They played it with the media that they are most at home with and that, of course, is the record. I think in the near future, we will see a resurrection of Paul McCartney; we will see a lot of publicity given to the fact that he is indeed alive and kicking. I'm overwhelmed by the intensity of thought that has gone into this and I'm also overwhelmed by the idea that the general public has taken this long to catch on to the Beatle game...or the Beatle Plot, if you will.

XXI.

"America! America! You Want To Believe In Miracles So Hard, Look What You're Willing To Do To Paul McCartney."
—Alfred Aronowitz,
The New York Post (October 25, 1969)

The youth of 1969 lived in a sort of yin/yang era. The late sixties were at the same time an Age of Enlightenment and an Age of Despair.

Half-a-million kids gathered at Woodstock during the summer of 1969 and proved to the world that a utopian nation could peacefully coexist with the Establishment. But six months later, those illusions came tumbling down with the disastrous and violent proceedings at Altamont (the Rolling Stones' own attempt to recreate Utopia).

The conservatism of the McCarthy-era fifties was cast away like a red satin dress as the new generation boldly skinny-dipped in the Sexual Revolution. The water, however, wasn't clean enough to drink; the pollution of the planet had become an almost insurmountable problem.

Mankind had finally broken the bonds of earth and had set foot on another celestial body. But the wonders of the Moon Landing couldn't disguise the fact that right here on earth a foreign war was senselessly claiming the lives of thousands of young Americans.

With so many confusing stimuli, young people needed a stable force upon which to focus. Pragmatism was the order of the day; teenagers and young adults questioned the standard religious systems in which their parents placed their faith. John Lennon was correct in 1966 when he stated that the Beatles were more popular than Jesus Christ; in a way, the Beatles had become the new messiahs and their songs were the words of the new gods. Forget heaven and hell; all you needed was love. "The love you take is equal to the love you make"—the equation exhibited Christ-like beauty in its simplicity.

So, many sought a secular explanation for life and the Beatles were the explainers. The popular *San Francisco Chronicle*

columnist Ralph J. Gleason saw the "Paul-is-Dead" phenomenon as an outgrowth of this theological thought. "They've got
it all wrong," wrote Gleason,* "it's God that's dead, not Paul
McCartney. No one believes in anything anymore and man has
a deep need to believe. Remove his objects of belief and he will
invent others. The Beatles are only part of it, but an important
part. They have become secular saints and, in absence of personal manifestations in Candlestick Park or elsewhere, free
imaginative play occurs which invents mythology to fill a void."

Like Jesus Christ, the Beatles were archetypes and they
had a large number of fervent followers. "The Beatles were very
important in a lot of people's lives," reflects Fred LaBour today.
"When they changed, we perceived change in ourselves. They
were enormous cultural icons to that whole generation that was
coming of age then. What happened to them mattered drasti-
cally to all of us."

LaBour realized the theological aspect of the rumor even
as he wrote his *Michigan Daily* article. He proposed that Lennon
was creating a new religion based around the death and subsequent resurrection of McCartney. Although tongue was lodged
firmly in cheek, large segments of LaBour's thesis became a
litany within the "Paul-is-Dead" rumor as it spread from Ann
Arbor to Detroit to New York to London. Along the way, the
origin of this quasi-religion became vague. Unaware that Fred
LaBour had single-handedly created the fictitious religion in
the name of satire, the cluesters simply accepted it as common
knowledge.

Sociological discussions began to appear in print. *Time*
magazine published an essay entitled "Of Rumor, Myth and a
Beatle." It suggested a reason allegorical to Gleason's for the
spread of the rumor: "Those who believe that McCartney is dead
are in part sublimating their fear of the grave. For whenever
death visits another person, it must delay its appointment with
you."

Fear of death was a big part of the McCartney rumor and,

---

*"Secular 'Saints' and a New Mythology," by Ralph J. Gleason, *San
Francisco Chronicle* (November 5, 1969)

correspondingly, a big part of religion. Hunting for clues was fun, but an underlying component started to surface. The cluesters were transferring their own fears of death to someone who was better equipped to handle it. Paul was the perfect recipient for this catharsis. He was hugely successful, utterly handsome, bigger than life—in fact, he had been elevated to superhuman status. The idea that McCartney could be dead but still exist became an accepted cornerstone of the theory. The rumor spread without grief because a deity like Paul could surely handle death.

Artifacts culled from various Eastern and Western religions were cast into this new theology. Resurrection was borrowed from Christianity; certain backwards messages such as "I shed the light" (reportedly found on "Your Mother Should Know") echoed Buddhist thought. A melting pot of spiritual beliefs produced a very potent stew; Paul's death could be proved one way or another. A walrus may have meant nothing when viewed through Judeo-Christian eyes but, in a certain ancient Viking mythology, the walrus was a symbol of death. The Beatles were worldly and they knew about all religions, said the cluesters. Certainly, they expected the same intellectual scrutiny from their fans.

As Russ Gibb surmised during the WKNR radio documentary, religion and the Beatles had crossed paths before. In 1966, John Lennon had remarked to Maureen Cleave of the *London Evening Standard* that Christianity seemed to him to be on the wane. "Christianity will go," Lennon stated. "It will vanish and shrink. I needn't argue about that, I'm right and will be proved right. We're more popular than Jesus Christ now. I don't know which will go first, rock 'n' roll or Christianity."

In Great Britain, these remarks were shrugged off as a typical pithy Lennonism, but when the interview was reprinted several months later in the U.S. teen publication *Datebook*, the problems for Lennon and the Beatles began. In particular, the "Bible-Belt" found Lennon's comments extremely offensive, and Southern radio stations began to sponsor Beatle Bonfires and Beatle Boycotts. Church leaders decried the band from the pulpits and the congregations responded by burning Beatles record albums (actually, only the covers; the toxic fumes from smoldering discs proved too great a risk. The vinyl was stomped upon instead).

Then-manager Brian Epstein flew to America in an attempt to douse the fires, but was rebuffed. Lennon finally arrived and tried to explain that his remarks were taken out of context. He was only commenting on the loss of interest in religion, he said. The civic leaders couldn't have cared less about Lennon's motives, and badgered him into admitting he was wrong. He reluctantly apologized for the trouble he had caused and was, for the most part, forgiven. The embarrassment of the entire episode, however, stayed with Lennon for the rest of his career.

Was the "Paul-is-Dead" rumor, then, a rebuttal by Lennon for the humiliation he suffered at the hands of the bible-thumping right-wing society? Many individuals from the Beatle Hoax Faction thought so. To them, this would explain the attire Lennon chose to wear on the cover of the **Abbey Road** album. Lennon's white preacher's suit conveyed a certain self-awareness of his place with the schematic of the new religion. And McCartney, barefoot and close-eyed, represented the Christ figure, resurrected from the grave.

Lennon denied that he had anything to do with the rumor and continued to deny his involvement, right up to his death in 1980. He most likely was speaking the truth, for no other reason than the fact that he would have revelled in the knowledge that he had pulled off the most fantastic hoax in history. He would certainly want to let the world know about it.

In 1969, however, no such hindsight was available. The accusations fell hard and heavy upon the Beatles organization and Lennon could do nothing to change the opinions of the Beatle Hoax Faction. "I'm much older and much wiser now," David Lock says with a laugh, "but back then, I was sure [Lennon] was having his say about the stupidity of the rednecks who blew his 'Christ' remark out of proportion. I never thought Paul was dead, really, but I thought Lennon engineered his death to make fun of Christianity." Lock, a former student of a Midwestern university, still found it enjoyable to search for clues. "It was a great game, or whatever, and we all did it at my school. Occasionally, I still like to listen for 'I buried Paul' at the end of 'Strawberry Fields Forever.'"

"The Mike Douglas Show," one of the most popular syndicated entertainment programs of its time, couldn't resist involving itself in the controversy. On a show in late October, the British comedy troupe The Scaffold made an appearance to promote their tour of the States. They performed five delightful skits and then sat down to chat with the host.

"I enjoyed you very much, gentlemen," Douglas said. "I understand one of you is the brother of Paul McCartney—which one is it?"

The three men on the couch who had introduced themselves as Michael McGear, John Gorman and Roger McGough began glancing at each other and goofing with Douglas. "Really? Which one?"

"No, really, seriously," Mike Douglas smiled and cast an eye to the man furthest away on the couch. "You, the young man in the leather jacket?"

Michael McGear nodded. "Yeah, it's me."

"Well, I want to compliment you for not using the same last name."

"Yeah, well, it would've been obvious. You don't want to cash in on somebody that famous."

Douglas turned toward the camera. "We have a young man to bring out right now. Of course, you've been reading a lot about Beatle Paul McCartney. He's been the center of quite a bit of controversy the past few weeks and, of course, the question 'is Paul McCartney dead?' has made headlines across the United States and, I'm sure, the world." The host then introduced his next guest. WNEW documentary producer Christopher Glenn appeared on the set, armed with a stack of Beatles albums. The Scaffold eyed him with contempt as he took a seat next to Douglas.

"Welcome, Chris. Just to fill everyone in, explain what this is all about."

Glenn proceeded to explain the theory. He pointed out a

few of the clues in the **Magical Mystery Tour** booklet and on the cover of **Sgt. Pepper.** Some of the audio clues were played over the public address system. McGear and the rest of Scaffold listened to, but mostly laughed at, Glenn's presentations. When Mike Douglas asked for McGear's thoughts on the rumor, he lashed out with venom.

"First off, I find it really embarrassing what you were just saying," McGear pointed a finger at Glenn, "but the worst thing was that it was boring. For the last—however long that took— was a very boring piece of television. You've got nothing at all to base it on. It's all a fantastically-contrived piece of press material of which you're making a television debut."

Douglas tried to steer the conversation away from personal attack. "Do you call that a hoax, Michael?"

"No, I think he's dead all right." The studio audience erupted in laughter. McGear became serious again. "No, it's really terrifying that you get away with it."

Glenn appeared to be fidgeting uncomfortably in his chair. Still, he retained his professional reserve. He was, after all, only reporting on a news event. "I think that it is absurd to assume that Paul is dead," Glenn replied. "The thing that interests me is the way America has responded to this absurd rumor of Paul McCartney's death—"

"Don't you see," McGear interrupted, "you're assisting that rumor and advancing it."

"I didn't make it up," Glenn calmly replied, "and I'm not advancing it either."

McGear leaned forward on the couch. "Even *not* making it up, you're still perpetrating [sic] the whole thing, sort of keeping it going." Glenn was dumbfounded and sat silently as Mike Douglas picked up the conversation.

"When was the last time you saw your brother?"

"The last time?" McGear responded quizzically.

"Yes."

"It was his funeral, I think." Once again, the audience roared with laughter.

Douglas laughed along with everyone and then redirected his question. "Really, when was the last time?"

McGear shrugged his shoulders. "I don't know—I mean, before I came, you know."

"Well, that was fairly recently, then?"

Roger McGough nudged McGear with his elbow. "Didn't look well, though, did he, Mike?"

"No," replied the straight-faced McGear, "he had a black arm-band on, with O.P.D. and he said, 'I'm dead, I'm dead.'" There was more laughter.

The show soon went to a commercial and the guests were escorted backstage. As Glenn gathered his materials together, McGear approached and began to once again chide him for his dissertation on stage. "So how much cash have you made off of this so far, mate?"

Glenn, free from the cameras and lights, finally let his emotions out. "Listen, buddy," he shouted, shaking his finger in McGear's face, "I didn't make a dime off of your brother's alleged death." Seeing the shocked expression on McGear's face, he dropped his finger and regained his composure. "Look, I'm a reporter. I'm just presenting this as a sociological phenomenon. It's news, that's all. I'm not trying to cause a sensation."

McGear looked as if he was going to respond, but then simply turned and walked back to his dressing room.

THE GUARDIAN

London   Thursday October 23 1969   6d

A CUT ABOVE THE REST
DRUMMON
FREEDOM SUIT

battle
British
nists

● JACKSON

will meet in congress next month in faced. For the first time, there is the ae party leaders, and with it the chance fficials and Mr R. Palme Dutt, probably nong the opponents of the leadership. evolt centres is the reaction of the British f Czechoslovakia. But it has become clear pate among party members that the differ-signs that the rebels are receiving active

tion of the extent of the split is that it has ty's own journal. It reached its peak when publicly urged party members to reject otion endorsing

adopted on a by the party's mmittee.

nted out that 40 he votes on the ar's district con-lled to support the—which con-ussian interven-r party members to me that this ld be up to 50

quoted

situation without

mentary on the Czech resolu-tion the Surrey committee says : " Czechoslovakia is men-tioned, but only to endorse every word in the executive committee statements which so bitterly divided our party, were so contrary to most other parties, and which according to Comrade Husak the Czech leader who succeeded Mr Dubcek] were based on 'super-ficial knowledge.' A fresh assessment is required which takes into account all that has happened including the recent statements of the Czechoslovak leaders."

The Beatles and I ——By VICTOR KEE

RUMOURS that Paul McCartney is dead, which have pushed the Beatles back to the top of the charts in America, are only part of a new surge of Beatlemania which is sweeping across the United States. I know because, unfortunately, my tele-phone has proved an all too 'accurate barometer of the Beatles' popularity in the United States.

Hundreds of people have rung my number day and night from America, where it has a magical significance, asking to speak to characters associated with Beatle songs. This has built up to a cres-cendo in recent days.

Courteous

" Hallo, can I speak to Ser-geant J. Pepper," says a typi-cal voice, courteous, charming — and with the charges reversed.

For months I bravely lost nervous energy in an attempt to discover the secret of why all America wanted to ring me. Late at night I would awake as if in the midst of a nightmare and reach shak-

● LEFT : the victim—otherwise, Victor Keegan, the " Guardian's " Industrial Correspondent. BELOW : the clue, reversed

ingly for the telephone to hear : " I have a collect call for Mr Billy Shears from Chicago, Illinois. Will you accept ? "

No calls were accepted, but as they grew more numerous and the American operators more intrigued (I am almost on Christian name terms with some of them), it turned out that I was being rung because of rumours that if you rang a magic number concealed on the sleeve of the " Magical Mystery Tour" album you would be able to hear the Beatles, be translated to mysterious romantic lands, and various other refinements.

The resurgence of Beatle-mania in the States is now taking teenagers on a magical mystery tour, courtesy of Bell Telephone, which ends icono-clastically at my telephone number.

A girl from California, who did not transfer the charges (she will have to learn the hard way), said she dis-covered me through gazing at the word Beatles, written in stars on the album sleeve, reversing the image in the mirror, and then reading backwards.

If you screw your eyes up a bit, and let your imagina-tion roam after a few scotches you can just about squeeze

my number, 834 7132, out of it. See the picture below—and if you still do not believe this, hundreds of teenagers and others do.

Most of the callers ask for Billy or Mr William] Shears, who appears on the Beatles' Sergeant Pepper LP, though why they ask for him especi-ally I have never discovered. Others ask for Mr Kite, Mr Henderson (" The Hendersons will all be there "), Ivor Cutler, George Martin, Derek Taylor, and other less familiar names.

John Lennon, Paul McCart-ney, and George Harrison are frequently asked for, but never Ringo . . . Now that's the stuff real rumours are made of.

Off hook

The nightly dialogue is con-ducted with callers in Chicago, New York, California, Florida, and a host of other States. Over the past few days, as rumours of Paul's death (denied categorically by Apple in London) have mounted, the telephone would have been ringing almost con-tinuously if it were not off the hook.

Most people want to hear that Paul is alive (asking through the operator) and once I confirm that, they refuse to believe that they have come through to the wrong number. One caller asked if Paul was alive and then added : " Can you give me any information about the R and D mortuary."

Yesterday, before leaving for work, I put the telephone back on the hook and it rang almost immediately. A voice with a Southern drawl said : " Hallo, sir, this is John K. Roberts, Radio Corporation of Miami, Florida. Can you tell me and my listeners if Paul McCartney is alive ? " And so on and so on.

My favourite was Jane from Milwaukee, whom I shall miss

dearly. She had tri bination 834 713 American exchang me : " I was sitting puzzling the quiz o suddenly realised number must be a She cooled noticeal me when I confe not a Beatle, but fo though how they wh was.

In spite of mont tioning I have bee trace the origin mythology of my number. Most peo think it was starte local radio station spread like a fores only common link is the consistent us song language (" Paul died Wednesd at five o'clock ?")

Most callers sour self-confident, not little " high," unapologetic about on a transferred ch in the middle of On the rare occas been able to get about how they ca for a telephone the album, they u " Oh I got it from mine."

Severe

Yesterday my m tery tour ended. V ing of relief, I slightly with regr decided to get n changed, severing a transatlantic link been with me on many months.

I rang the supervisor expec sympathy for my nights. Instead sh to be thrilled to " That's marvellous " You should be that story to the for a fortune."

Alas, the unknow of being a reporter.

XXII.
"We Get Letters From All Sorts Of Nuts, But Paul Is Still Very Much With Us."
—An unidentified spokesman from Apple Records

WMCA's disc jockey, Alex Bennett, was still in London searching for McCartney. Unaware that the musician had made an exodus to Scotland with *Life* magazine in hot pursuit, Bennett continued to scour the city for Paul or anyone who knew him. Although his mission was purely in the spirit of a large-scale scavenger hunt, Bennett had some serious thoughts about the event. "The only way McCartney is going to quell the rumors," he told *The New York Times*, "is by coming up with a set of fingerprints from a 1965 passport which can be compared to his current prints. Otherwise, people will suspect either that the story is true, or that the story is being used as promotion by Apple—and that would hurt the Beatles' image."

The main office of Apple Records was still receiving hundreds of phone calls a day, virtually jamming the switchboards and making normal business operations impossible. But Apple wasn't the only recipient of unusual phone calls in London. Several regular customers had the phone company change their numbers because they were tired of taking calls from strangers in search of clues. According to the *London Express*, one man was repeatedly asked if he was Brian Epstein (the Beatles' late manager). Another man picked up the phone only to hear, "Billy Shears told me to call."

Victor Keegan, a correspondent with *The Guardian*, discovered that his phone number—834-7132 —also held a particular mystic significance to Beatles fans. "Hundreds of people have rung my number day and night from America," Keegan wrote in the October 23 issue of his newspaper, "asking to speak to characters associated with Beatle songs. This has built up to a crescendo in recent days." The journalist also indicated that he, too, asked the phone company to change his number.

Apparently, all of these individuals' telephone numbers corresponded to digits that were allegedly contained on the cover of the Beatles' **Magical Mystery Tour** album. Depending on whether the front jacket was held upside-down or read from the reflection in a mirror, any one of a series of numbers would reveal itself to the cluesters. 834-7132 was a frequent result, as well as 537-1038, 834-7135, and 837-1438. Residents in both the United States and Great Britain realized in the final weeks of October that there were few things worse than owning one of these telephone exchanges.

It was from this "secret phone number" that a rumor suddenly sprang from the rumor. According to the *Washington Evening Star* (October 25, 1969), and additionally cited in several other newspapers, a story had begun to make the rounds at more than a few universities. It suggested that a certain student at Northwestern University held the **Magical Mystery Tour** album upside down and discovered the name "BEATLES" became a seven-digit phone number. He dialed the number and reached someone who began to quiz him on Beatles trivia. When the student answered all of the questions correctly, he was told he had won a trip to Pepperland.

A few days later, an envelope arrived in the mail. Inside were Pepperland tickets and a short note instructing the student to lick the outside of the stamp on the envelope. He did so, and soon found himself on an LSD trip. Believing himself to be imbibed with mystical Beatle powers, the student opened the window of his dorm room and leapt out. He fell five stories to his death.

Several journalists, including Mike Oberman of the *Evening Star*, sought out documentation of this fantastic story but, like all good urban legends, the mythical student could never be located. Other variations of this story had the student receiving the tickets with instructions to go to a secluded location where a U.F.O. in the form of a Yellow Submarine greeted him and whisked him away to Pepperland. Still another legend told of three friends who all won trips. They spent the next couple of days telling their classmates about the contest. And then they mysteriously vanished without a trace.

There were many cluesters who maintained that there was a secret code to be cracked and that a journey to a secret Beatles hideaway would be the reward. John Summer, the clue expert of Ohio Wesleyan, had finished a late class one evening in early November and was walking back to his apartment. As he approached, he could make out a human form sitting on the front stoop. It was twilight, but Summer saw that it was a young man with long, stringy hair and a thick brown mustache. He was dressed in ragged blue jeans and had an olive drab duffel bag perched across his lap.

"Hey, man," the stranger slurred slowly, "you're John Summer, right?"

Summer cautiously approached the man as he rose clumsily to his feet. The duffel bag tumbled to the ground. John stared into the man's bloodshot eyes and replied, "Yeah, that's right."

The stranger offered his hand in greeting. "I'm Ace from Bakersfield, man. I came to ask you a question."

Summer began to feel a little uneasy. Here was some weird guy who came all the way from California to no doubt talk to him about the McCartney clues. The whole thing was getting too freaky; it wasn't fun anymore. Only two days ago, he had received a death threat over the phone. And now, here he was, face-to-face with a real scary character.

"John, man, I got all the info I need," Ace said as he pulled a spiral notebook from his bag, "'cept I need to know from you how to complete this one phrase." Summer looked at the open page of the notebook and saw a collection of drawings and letter groups. "Y'see, John, man," Ace continued, "you break up the name 'BEATLES' and it says 'BE AT LES,' but I don't know where 'LES' is. Is it an abbreviation or something? Can you help me so I can get to the Land of Yellow Submarines?"

Summer numbly shook his head. "I don't know anything about that. I really don't..."

Ace appeared crestfallen. "I thought you were the expert, man. I read about you in the paper." He brought the notebook closer to Summer. "I need to find out. My friend figured it out and he's there, man. I gotta get there, too."

Summer moved to the door and unlocked it. "I really don't know," he repeated as he slipped inside. "Look, I have to go."

Ace stared vacantly at Summer and finally uttered, "Man,

I thought you could help." He picked up his duffel bag and strode into the darkness. John Summer watched him walk away and felt the lump in his stomach soften. "That does it," he said to himself, "I'm getting out of this thing."

He shut the door to his apartment and, at the same time, shut the door on his participation with the "Paul-is-Dead" rumor. It would be years before he ever discussed it again.

XXIII.
"Do I Look Dead? I'm As Fit As A Fiddle."
—Paul McCartney,
to a reporter from the British newspaper *The People*.

After the unexpected visit from *Life* magazine, Paul McCartney decided his self-imposed seclusion was causing more trouble than it was worth. When a reporter from the BBC appeared at the Scottish farmhouse on the afternoon of October 26, Paul invited him inside for an interview without hesitation.

"I think the main thing is I haven't enjoyed really doing interviews and getting a lot of publicity lately," McCartney explained. "I've preferred just to sort of sit here more in the background to be more with the family.

"So, I think that probably started the thing, because I used to do maybe an interview a week just to keep my name in the headlines. Well, I'm going through a phase now where I don't want to be in the limelight."

"I just think it ruins our life," wife Linda chimed in. "I don't think people realize that to them, it's headlines in the newspapers, but everybody starts bothering us. We came out here on a holiday to be left alone."

"I'm not going to try to spoil people's fantasies," Paul continued, "but if the conclusion they reach is that I'm dead, then they're wrong. Because I'm alive and living in Scotland."

The interview was taped and segments appeared that evening on BBC radio. Newspapers in the United States also reprinted the interview the following day.

Over the course of the next few days, McCartney granted more interviews. After correspondent Hugh Farmer of *The People* got past Paul's watchdog neighbor John MacDougall ("When I approached, John shouted and bawled as my car wheels spun in the mud, to make it clear I had to go no farther, and that no one was going near his V.I.P. neighbor"), he and McCartney chatted about the rumor.

"Tell them how you have found me," Paul pleaded, "very much alive. I haven't bothered trying to crush [the rumor] until now because I quite honestly believe I have no obligation to put right the wrongs other people have created."

McCartney, for the first time, tried to thoughtfully de-bunk some of the clues. In response to the furor over the **Abbey Road** cover, he told Farmer: "I appeared on a record sleeve in bare feet because, frankly, when those pictures were taken it was so hot I was too warm to wear shoes." About the O.P.D. on his Sgt. Pepper uniform, he said, "I don't know what it means. I got it from a Canadian policeman." And the black carnation on the **Magical Mystery Tour** album?—"I was wearing a black flower...because after the lads got their red ones there wasn't one left for me."*

Apparently determined to put the rumor to rest, he once again became accessible to the press. It was a turning point in the drama. The rumor, which had spread like wildfire with McCartney's silence, began to recede with his reemergence in the public.

While some still maintained that a double was doing the Beatles' bidding and others were sure it was a group-inspired hoax, most of the kids conceded that the game was over. At Hofstra University, Lewis Yager's *Is Paul McCartney Dead Society* called its final meeting. After an agreement that no more could be accomplished in light of recent developments, the com-mittee was dissolved. Other campuses across the country also began to slowly return to normal.

"I think reality began to set in," suggests Marilyn Denbloch, a former Eastern Michigan University student. "The clue hunt took our minds off of the really scary things that were going on around us, but then we had to face up to life."

"There was a war in Vietnam," adds another EMU alum-nus, "and it was quite possible that my friends and I could be drafted. Paul's death rumor sort of transferred our fears for awhile. But then we had to eventually look our fear straight in the eyes."

The Vietnam War had continued to loom large in the background during the rumor's circulation and, by the middle of

---

*"'Tell my Fans I'm Alive and Well!' Says Paul McCartney," by Hugh Farmer, *The People* (October 26, 1969).

November, it had strong-armed its way back to the forefront of consciousness. Rallies and demonstrations against America's involvement in the conflict recaptured the attention of students across the country. Beatles albums were filed away, while draft cards were pulled out of wallets to be tossed into the raging bonfire of public dissent.

President Nixon returned to the headlines and an out-of-work musician named Charles Manson was arrested for the Tate-LaBianca murders. A trial was underway in Chicago for Abbie Hoffman and six others charged with inciting a riot at the 1968 Democratic Convention. Love was still free, and grass was still meant to be smoked. Life on campus in 1969 was definitely the way it had always been, but, in essence, the course of the era had begun to change. When national guardsmen opened fire on Vietnam protesters at Kent State University, the bodies of four students became a sad legacy.

When the Beatles announced their demise in April of 1970, the period known as the sixties also came to an end. It was a short decade; many felt the term was bookended by the Beatles' existence. 1964 was the dawn and 1969 was the dusk. Such was the band's immense influence upon the culture that it is doubtful the world will ever again experience an event similar to the "Paul-is-Dead" rumor. The complexities of the story were reflections of a unique and confusing time in American history. Never again will so many diverse elements combine to create a breeding ground fertile enough to grow a grapevine as tangled and extensive.

Rumors come and go. Today, most of them end up on the pages of the less-than-reliable tabloid newspapers with little or no comment offered by the mainstream press. Occasionally, a story like the "Elvis is Alive" rumor of the late eighties will generate a degree of excitement, but the world at large seems to be a bit more wary of the implications of belief.

Russ Gibb agrees. "It seems to me that there's a great fascination that we had been duped. Could we be angry that we were part of the gag and didn't know about it? We don't want to be suckered again."

Gibb believes that the mass media were more than a little responsible for the spread of the rumor. "I don't trust the media, and I include myself in that. Remember, I was a promoter, and [my] sense of what made good copy was always working there. The media reads the media. We read what one another says and what one another writes."

On October 23, 1969, NBC correspondent John Chancellor ended the night's newscast by stating, "All we can report with certainty is that Paul McCartney is either dead or alive." When recently reminded of his statement, Chancellor chuckled and responded, "Oh, what a prudent thing I did!"

Asked for his thoughts on the role of the media in dealing with rumors, Chancellor said, "The one thing I've learned is that this is a very big church with a lot of chapels in it and a lot of people in many different pews. The only way you can understand the press is not to understand it...the press is like fire or water; it just can get out of control. And if you put in things like the McCartney rumor, you'll find that the press goes off in ninety-five different directions. I celebrate its diversity and I mourn its imperfections."

The total number of newspaper articles written about the rumor exceeded three hundred. While nearly all of them dealt with the story in a sober manner, many of them could not avoid a sensationalistic headline to draw attention. "Dead Or Alive?" asked a headline in *The Washington Daily* (October 21, 1969). *The Delaware Gazette* (October 23) wondered in its banner, "Was It Paul Who Called Detroit?" The campus newspapers also cast away good journalistic policy in order to titillate their readers with an unadorned "Is Paul Dead?" (*The Ohio State Lantern* and a half-dozen others). Clearly, the media carried a certain accountability for the spread of the rumor. It was an accountability that is not likely to be repeated in the foreseeable future.

One element of the "Paul-is-Dead" rumor does continue to flourish, however. Certain segments of the public continue to believe that rock 'n' roll bands insert secret messages into their recordings. The game, though, has become vulgar in its inferences.

It was not much of a game at all to the members of Judas

Priest. They were hauled into court during the summer of 1990 and charged in a product liability suit. Specifically, they were tried for contributing to the suicides of two young men in Nevada. The prosecution contended that a Judas Priest song entitled, "Better By You, Better Than Me" contained a backwards subliminal message which suggested: "...try suicide...let's be dead...do it, do it, do it." Two teenagers, Raymond Belknap and James Vance, reportedly listened to the song for several hours, over and over, while smoking marijuana and drinking beer. They then went to a nearby playground and turned a shotgun on themselves. Belknap died immediately, while Vance survived his injuries for three excruciating years. It was Vance's assertion to his mother before his death that suggested a criminal responsibility on the part of the band.

Early in the one month trial, William Nickloff Jr., an expert witness for the prosecution, demonstrated the presumption of hidden messages by playing the offending song forward, backward and at different speeds. He claimed to have located all of the alleged phrases, but those in the courtroom had a difficult time hearing them.

Another witness testified that she used a computer to examine the suspicious passages and also found evidence of subliminal messages. Judge Jerry Whitehead, presiding over the non-jury trial, was not convinced by the presentation and elected to rule for a dismissal of the charges. "They failed to prove that the defendants intentionally placed subliminal messages on the album and that those messages were a cause [in the suicides]," the judge wrote in his ninety-three-page ruling. Whitehead further indicated that "the words 'do it' are the result of a chance combination of sounds; the words were not intentionally formed."

Judas Priest and their record label (CBS) may have escaped prosecution, but this episode does not bode well for the future of the industry. By allowing the lawsuit to be tried in the first place, a dangerous precedent has been set, thus allowing similar cases to come to trial.

"This will not be the last case," predicted Kenneth McKenna, the attorney for the Belknap family. "There will be others and sooner or later someone will win."* One day, the judgement may indeed go to the plaintiffs—and this would be a tragedy.

While we have seen the power of the medium called the record album and the excitement created by (alleged) hidden audio information, it is laughable that anyone could believe a self-destructive action could be directed by language in a song. The suicides in the Priest case were the result of disturbed minds—emotional problems wholly separate from the music of a heavy metal band.

But why should we be surprised?

Parents have been blaming rock 'n' roll for all the evils in the world ever since the day Elvis Presley first gyrated his hips to the rhythm of "All Shook Up."

---

*United Press International, August 24, 1990.

XXIV.
"I Managed To Stay Alive Through It."
—Paul McCartney,
in a *Rolling Stone* interview (Jan. 31, 1974)

The "Paul-is-Dead" rumor started mysteriously and ended abruptly. Today, it is regarded as the ultimate example of fan worship, in that no other entertainer has been significant enough to generate a death rumor of such scope. It is doubtful that, even with purposeful intent, such an event could ever happen again. It was a mixture of the time and the powerful persona that brought about this incredible piece of rock history.

But was it more than a rumor? Today, more than twenty years after the fact, some still believe the whole thing was a hoax perpetrated by the Beatles themselves.

"To this day, I believe that there were *moments* and they can deny it until the end, but there were *moments,*" Russ Gibb stated recently. Today, the long brown mane is gone, replaced by a haircut which is both shorter and grayer. Now a sexagenarian, Gibb hasn't lost any of his youthful energy and he continues to work at several projects simultaneously. He's recognizable to many in the Dearborn area as the irreverent host of a cable talk show, "Russ Gibb At Random." He continues to teach broadcast journalism at Dearborn High School and bursts with the pride of a new father when he speaks of one of his "kids" who has gone on to success in the television industry. When Beatles-related conventions breeze into town, Gibb can usually be found there as a guest speaker, retelling the events that led him to his place in rock history.

And, as of this writing, Russ Gibb can still be found on the radio. He plays vintage Detroit rock 'n' roll once a week at WCSX-FM on a show he calls "Russ Gibb's Rock Chronicles." When the show debuted in April of 1988, Gibb devoted the first hours to a "Paul-is-Dead" retrospective. During the course of the program, Gibb received a phone call from a man who claimed he was the original "Tom" who contacted Uncle Russ on that fateful Sunday afternoon in 1969.

So how important is the "Paul-is-Dead" rumor in terms of

RUSS GIBB TODAY
Russ Gibb hosting "Rock Chronicles" on WCSX-FM.
Who knows who might call....
(Photo by Andru Reeve, from the author's collection.)

FRED LABOUR TODAY
Fred LaBour (left) reminisces with the author about his part
in the "Paul-is-Dead" rumor.
(Photo by Keith Allen, from the author's collection.)

history? "This rumor is like an ice crystal on a giant snow ball," Gibb postulates. "In the history of rock 'n' roll, I think that's all it is. But there is a sense that it was something bigger. Well, look, twenty years later, we're talking about it. Now, two thousand years from now if they're still talking about it, then I'll realize it was something."

And what became of University of Michigan sophomore Fred LaBour? Today, he's one-third of the humorous Western music trio, Riders In The Sky. Under the apt stage name of Too Slim, LaBour plays the stand-up bass and performs with the band throughout the United States and Canada. Riders In The Sky record for CBS Records and also present a weekly radio program ("Riders Radio Theatre") which is nationally-syndicated on public stations. In the fall of 1991, the band launched a Saturday morning children's TV show, "Harmony Ranch," broadcast nationwide on the CBS network.

LaBour's newspaper article, so pivotal to the spread of the "Paul-is-Dead" rumor, was intended as a satirical jab at the school of rock criticism. Nevertheless, more than two decades later, LaBour contends that there are obvious clues on Beatles albums.

"I don't think that the Beatles tried to start it," he explains, "[but] I think they had fun with it once it got going. You know, 'here's another clue for you all, the Walrus was Paul.' It's real Lennonesque."

Does he have any regrets about the episode? "I'm still a prankster," LaBour says as a sly smile fills his face, "and I'm liable to do it again, if the right situation comes up. It would have nothing to do with this, but..."

John Summer, the former Ohio Wesleyan student, has also chosen a career in the limelight. He's one of the evening news anchors on WTOG television in St. Petersburg, Florida. "The conclusion that I reached [in 1969] was that John Lennon was playing games," Summer said recently. "He was the major force behind the Beatles—its true soul and energy—and he always loved a good joke. I still do not know, however, if this was a joke."

FRED LaBour with Riders in the Sky
Fred "Too Slim" LaBour (left) is still horsing around as a member
—with "Ranger Doug" (center) and "Woody Paul" (right)—
of the humorous Western music trio Riders in the Sky.
(Photo by Don Putnam, courtesy Riders in the Sky.)

JOHN SUMMER TODAY
John Summer, shown
above on the cover of a
1990 issue of *Broadcast-
ing* magazine, is now a
news anchor at WTOG-
TV in Tampa/St. Peters-
burg, Florida.
O, Sweet Irony....
(Photo courtesy
John Summer/WTOG-TV.)

Lewis Yager, the former president of the *Is Paul McCartney Dead Society* at Hofstra University, resurfaced in 1979 with a self-produced radio show entitled, "Clues Revisited Ten Years Later." Armed with a decade of hindsight and still convinced that Lennon had engineered a hoax, Yager offered a very intriguing theory as to why he thought the clues were intentionally placed on the record albums. He proposed that since music ran in ten- to eleven-year cycles (Big Band in the forties, Rock 'n' Roll in the fifties, Beatles in the sixties) and nothing substantial had arisen in the seventies, perhaps the rumor was a method to ensure continued success for the Beatles in the next decade. "What would have happened if some person, or someone involved in all this would have released these clues somehow in '73, '74?" Yager postulated on his show. "Assuming that the clues had been picked up and had the same publicity we received in 1969...the Beatles would have established themselves with a whole new consumer market."

Victor Keegan, the hapless industrial correspondent at *The Guardian* whose telephone number was said to be secreted on the cover of **Magical Mystery Tour,** never subscribed to such a notion. "The reaction in America was [that] a lot of people were lulled into this sort of false innocence about what had happened," Keegan says today. Still employed as an assistant editor at *The Guardian*—but in possession of a different home phone number—Keegan is aware of the powerful influence that the Beatles wielded in Great Britain, as well as the United States: "Because they were the first of their kind—the first British group to make it in the States—at the time it was a fantastic national uplifting...everyone followed it with great pride."

But despite the importance of the Beatles in British life, the "Paul-is-Dead" rumor never really took hold there. Victor Keegan implies that there is a very simple reason for this: "In England, we knew he wasn't dead anyway."

Although the fervor of the event has abated over the past twenty years, the "Paul-is-Dead" rumor makes an appearance every Halloween on radio stations throughout the country in the form of playful "documentaries."

One such "Paul-is-Dead" retrospective took place in October of 1978 on CFNY in Toronto. John Small joined host David Marsden for a lively discussion about WKNR's part in the rumor. Excerpts from the Gibb-Carlisle-Small "Beatle Plot" program were rebroadcast for the first time in nine years.

Even at this late date, Small was convinced that the Beatles had somehow been involved in the dissemination of the "clues." When the discussion rolled around to the O.P.D. patch on Paul McCartney's uniform from the **Sgt. Pepper** album, Marsden came to agree with Small. This was their eerie observation, as broadcast to the radio audience:

> MARSDEN: I remember at the time, when all of this was done, the one hole that I always felt there was in the theory was the O.P.D. thing and I knew that coming from the United States as the whole program originally did, that you may not have known that O.P.P. was in fact the Ontario Provincial Police. And that the crest that is on his sleeve is in actual fact an O.P.P. police crest. And I spoke to you this afternoon about that and we got out the **Sgt. Pepper** album...and suddenly, I realized that, in fact, the last "P" on the crest looks as though it has been doctored...

> SMALL: Yes.

> MARSDEN: It doesn't look like a crease in the clothing as my eye had originally thought. And...you actually knew what an "O.P.P." was nine years ago?

> SMALL: We had had that inclination because, of course, having broadcast that program in Detroit, our signal went almost to London, Ontario. So, we had a great deal of input from people from Windsor and the surrounding areas.

> MARSDEN: Yeah, but it is interesting that on the Sgt. Pepper LP—

> SMALL: It does not look like "O.P.P."

> MARSDEN: No, it actually looks as though someone has

135

—if you folks know anything about photography and what can be done with airbrushes and other assorted things like that—it's phenomenal what you can do with a photograph. And it looks as though the last "P" in O.P.P. has been doctored...

And, beginning in October 1989 (the twentieth anniversary of the rumor), the syndicated radio program "Reeling In The Years" has presented an annual celebration of the "Paul-is-Dead" mania in the form of an audio pastiche of clues and interviews. On the initial outing, host George Taylor Morris even confessed to his own gullibility during the heyday of the rumor: "Do you believe we actually believed all of this? Didn't you? Yes, I did—at least for a while...I actually remember telling friends that it was indeed a fact that McCartney was dead, and then I followed that up with the entire spectrum of clues to prove it. Silly boy."

Interest in the rumor has even permeated popular prime time television programs. The September 28, 1990 episode of NBC's "Quantum Leap" (entitled "November 25, 1969—The Leap Home") depicted the lead character, Sam Beckett, time-traveling back to his boyhood home. In one scene, Sam and his twelve-year-old sister Katey are sitting on the family porch, Sam idly strumming his acoustic guitar. Katey excitedly tells him that she and all her friends played the White Album backwards and found out that Beatle Paul McCartney is dead. Sam laughs and tells his sibling that Paul is alive and well, but that the Beatles are going to break up in about six months and Paul is going to go on to form his own band, Wings. He almost slips and reveals the tragic fate of John Lennon, but catches himself and finishes the scene by playing a poignant rendition of "Imagine."

The rumor itself even made a small ripple of a reappearance in 1980, when Paul was arrested in Japan for possession of marijuana. It was passed around in small circles that the reason he was held in jail for ten days was because his fingerprints did not match those on file in Japan from the Beatles' 1966 tour. This, of course, was not the case. He was eventually deported back to England with no criminal charges lodged against him.

And what of Paul McCartney today? He is, indeed, alive and well. In late 1990, he concluded a worldwide tour, his first in more than a decade. All of the shows featured a healthy dose of nostalgia, as Paul trotted out a dozen classic Beatles songs to the delight of the sold-out audiences.

During the tour, McCartney attended a news conference in Auburn Hills, Michigan on February 2, 1990. The last remark from a Detroit reporter was inevitable:

> REPORTER: Russ Gibb asked me to pass along to you when I got here the fact that the rumors of his premature death are indeed rumors and he's alive and well and teaching at Dearborn High School.

> PAUL: Oh, really? Good. Say hi for *me!*

XXV.
"America Is Such A Fanatical Place...
No Other Place In The World
Would Create That Sort Of Story."
—George Harrison,
to *The New York Post* (October 25, 1969)

The question remains: how did it all start? Thus far, we've seen how a disc jockey in Detroit and a handful of Midwestern college students used the media at hand to propagate the "Paul-is-Dead" theory across the country and the world. But who or what planted the original seed which grew into this immense network of grapevines? First of all, let's take a look back to London two-and-a-half years before the rumor rocked the rock world.

In the February 1967 issue of the *Beatles Book Monthly* (the official Beatles fanzine), there was a small article entitled, "False Rumour":

> Stories about the Beatles are always flying around Fleet Street. The seventh of January was very icy, with dangerous conditions on the Ml motorway, linking London with the Midlands, and towards the end of the day, a rumor swept London that Paul McCartney had been killed in a car crash on the Ml. But, of course, there was absolutely no truth in it at all, as the Beatles' Press Officer found out when he telephoned Paul's St. Johns Wood home and was answered by Paul himself who had been at home all day with his black Mini Cooper safely locked up in the garage.

Because the rumor had been nipped in the bud, no follow-up was offered by any of the national newspapers in London. Could this be the incident that initiated the whole affair nearly three years later? Was England actually responsible for a rumor that seemed to generate from the United States? While I believed this was the case when I began this project, my subsequent research has indicated that the true germ of the rumor is quite a bit more complex. Although the ironic article quoted above may have played a minor role in the larger drama, it is this author's presumption that the rumor did in fact have its

TERRY KNIGHT
Before Terry Knight created Grand Funk Railroad, he recorded
an enigmatic single for Capitol Records called "Saint Paul."
Did he inadvertently start the "Paul-is-Dead" rumor?
(Photo courtesy Detroit *Free Press*.)

genesis in Detroit. Let's return to Michigan and take another, closer, look at one of its former residents.

Terry Knight was something of a local celebrity in the Detroit region. Born Richard Terrence Knapp in Flint on April 9, 1943, Knight graduated from high school and almost immediately began working as a disc jockey at WFYC in Alma. He then moved on to spin records at WTAC and WJBK, before settling in at the Canadian border powerhouse CKLW in Windsor, Ontario. It was there he sealed his reputation as a top Detroit personality.

Although he had earned thousands of loyal teenaged fans, Knight was bitten by the British Invasion bug and he tendered his resignation at the end of 1964 to pursue a singing career. A trip to England bore no fruit, so Terry returned home to eke out a living as a folk singer and part-time disc jockey.

During a foray to a Flint nightclub, Knight happened upon a group called The Jazz Masters. He thought they were superb and he eventually convinced them to form a new group with him. With that, Terry Knight and the Pack were born.

The Pack held reign over the Detroit rock scene from 1965 to 1967. Their live performances at places like Russ Gibb's Grande Ballroom were sold out and their records received airplay on all of the local rock stations, including Knight's old haunt CKLW. (One of their early songs, "How Much More," is considered an underground classic, and has appeared on several compilations of sixties proto-punk.) With all of this attention, however, the Pack couldn't get the rest of the country to show more than a passing interest in the band. Only one of their recordings (a remake of the Ben E. King hit, "I Who Have Nothing") made a significant mark on the national charts. Additionally, bookings for the group rarely extended outside of the Midwest. After recording two albums for the Cameo-Parkway label, the band called it quits.

Terry Knight drifted around Detroit, a man without a band. He and his acoustic guitar played one-night stands in coffee houses for the rest of the year. Then one day in early 1968, Knight received a phone call from Paul McCartney, who requested a business meeting with him. It seemed that anorexic superstar Twiggy had toured with Knight and enjoyed his music. She was aware the Beatles were seeking out new talent to sign to their fledgling Apple Records label, so she tipped off her pal Paul. Knight caught the next flight to London and met with McCartney to discuss the possibilities of joining Apple, but he ended up declining the offer.*

Knight returned to Michigan, signed a limited recording deal with Capitol Records, and began to compose songs that had a more ethereal and expressive feel to them. During his meeting with McCartney, Knight became aware that all was not well in the Beatles' camp. Rumors had been circulating for months about the certainty of a break-up, and this gossip was supported by what he saw during his visit. Paul seemed to be the glue that was holding the group together. Creative inspiration hit Knight as he remembered his journey to Apple and he composed a song entitled, "Saint Paul."

Because the present holder of the copyright of "Saint Paul" (no longer Terry Knight) has refused to grant permission, it is impossible to reprint the entire lyric (seven four- and five-line stanzas). However, for the sake of exposition and to understand the song's possible connection to the "Paul-is-Dead" rumor, it would perhaps be beneficial to synopsize the song and take advantage of our "fair use" rights to quote a small portion of it.

At first glance, the bulk of the lyrics appear to be esoteric and largely meaningless; however, repeated readings tend to reveal many references to Apple Records' troubled business state ("Sir Isaac Newton said it'd have to fall," "While you and Sgt. Pepper saw the writing on the wall," and "You knew it all along/ Something had gone wrong"). On the other hand, there are also several vague stanzas at the beginning of the song, where the singer seems to be talking to Paul as if he (Paul) were a heavenly spirit). Below are the first two lines of the first stanza,

---

*This meeting was documented in a May 2, 1969 article in *The Detroit Free Press.*

and the last two lines of the second stanza:

> I looked into the sky
> Everything was high....

> Did I hear you call,
> Or was I dreaming then, Saint Paul?

While the song doesn't come right out and say that McCartney is dead, the preceding excerpts could certainly be interpreted that way. However, "Saint Paul" cannot be treated as just another "Paul-is-Dead" novelty song; as a song recorded and released to cash in on the prevalent and grisly rumor. Why not? Because "Saint Paul" was released on Capitol Records (2506) on May 19—a full five months before the rumor gained national prominence! *Billboard* magazine mentioned the song in its "Special Merit" section of the May 31 issue. It read as follows:

> Dedicated to Beatle Paul McCartney, Knight comes up with an unusual, original ballad loaded with underground appeal.

The song only made it to #114 on the *Billboard* charts, falling off around the first week of July. The only reason the song made it *that* far up the charts was because of the airplay it received in Knight's adopted hometown—Detroit!

But how could this song be the source of all which transpired the following fall? Knight obviously was making a comment about the apparently hopeless situation at Apple. Allen Klein, the New York attorney who had advised the Rolling Stones on their sagging financial condition, had been brought in to do the same for the Beatles. Klein's presence, in fact, was the main reason Knight had turned down a chance to record for Apple. (Klein operated the label that the Pack once recorded for and Knight wasn't pleased with the way the attorney had handled the royalties).

As Knight insinuated in his lyrics, Sir Isaac Newton said the Apple would fall. Certainly, this was a reference to the

"SAINT PAUL" RECORD LABEL
The single "Saint Paul" by Terry Knight, released five months
before the controversy, may have had a great deal to do with the
beginning of the rumor. Note the publisher of the song—Maclen Music
was Lennon and McCartney's publishing company!
(Photo from the author's collection.)

troubled business affairs within the Beatles' empire.

All in all, the song was deep and mystifying, much as
Billboard had described it. But what did the vacationing Midwest college kids think when they heard it over the course of the
summer?

"I remember that song," recounts Rick Sandherst, a former
Michigan student. "It was sort of strange and I wasn't sure
what it was about, but I liked it. The radio station played it a
couple of times, 'cause it was sung by the guy who used to jockey
[at that station]."

In the song, Knight refers to McCartney as "Saint Paul."
According to the dictionary, a saint is a person who is recognized
in Christian theology as being in heaven with God, while being
venerated by those on Earth. Could it be that a person like Rick

144

heard "Saint Paul," saw some interesting things on Beatles album sleeves, heard some death references in Beatles songs, and made some sort of connection? Upon returning to a nearby college campus after summer break, this person perhaps had the foundation of a theory which he shared with his friends. Clue-hunting and conjecture would follow and, eventually, Tim Harper would hear about the rumor from Dartanyan Brown and write that first newspaper account on September 17, 1969. After that, the rumor would reach "Tom" and he would make his historic phone call to Uncle Russ Gibb at WKNR.

It is very likely that the course of events followed the preceding outline. The rumor, however, cannot be dismissed as simply the result of an active and macabre imagination. It must be asked whether Terry Knight had a malicious objective in mind when he wrote and recorded "Saint Paul." Did he desire to start a death rumor? We may never know the answer to that question; Knight isn't talking. He remains incommunicado, refusing all requests for interviews. He may just want his privacy. He may still hold a grudge against the press for labeling him a megalomaniacal Svengali during his early seventies reign over Grand Funk Railroad. His headstrong attitude and tight-fisted control, in fact, got him sacked in 1973 and he faded from the rock scene.

There may, however, be something else to consider. Maybe Paul McCartney and the Beatles *did* have something to do with the rumor. Maybe Paul had talked Knight into composing "Saint Paul" when they met in 1968.

You see, the lyrics to "Saint Paul" were published by MacLen Music, Inc.—Lennon and McCartney's own publishing company!

MacLen Music, Inc. was set up in 1963 exclusively to publish the words and melodies of John Lennon and Paul McCartney. Even George Harrison and Ringo Starr were excluded from this publishing arm; they had their own companies to take care of their creations. So why would Knight's "Saint Paul" be administered by MacLen Music? Knight owned his own publishing company (Storybook Music) which he used for everything else he wrote or produced.

Within the structure of "Saint Paul," there are lyrical references to some of the Beatles' best-loved songs, but these are lyrical fragments or paraphrased allusions and they are not covered under copyright laws. The coda of the song *does* use the music from "Hey Jude," but this is noted separately on the record label. The bulk of Knight's song is highly original and, yet, it is administered in a blanket agreement with MacLen Music. Why?

The enigma of a Terry Knight song published by the Beatles' own company may be a bigger mystery than the "Paul-is-Dead" rumor itself. My letters and phone calls to all those principles involved have gone unanswered. The Library of Congress in Washington, D.C. confirms the information on the record label—"Saint Paul" somehow found its way into the same company as such Beatles classics as "Paperback Writer," "Lucy In the Sky With Diamonds," and "Let It Be."

The facts are there. We are left to speculate as to whether the song was inaugurated by the Beatles and, if not, why it ended up as a MacLen Music publication. And did this song in fact serve as the true catalyst of this fascinating rumor?

A conclusion cannot be drawn. With virtually any rumor, one can only ponder as to the cause or course. Unless someone steps forth to accept the credit (or the blame), we can only view the "Paul-is-Dead" rumor as a mysterious and eerie piece of rock 'n' roll history. For a few weeks in 1969, we were amateur sleuths, turning over the stones looking for clues. We were looking for answers in a time full of questions.

We were looking for a dead man to turn us on.

Epilogue

It was nearing Thanksgiving and the biting cold Detroit winter had begun to set in. Russ Gibb, his hands thrust deep into his coat pockets, pushed open the door to the WKNR studio with his shoulder. Once inside, he waved hello to the receptionist and proceeded to the lounge to check his messages.

Dan Carlisle was already in the lounge. He was hunched over a large cardboard box that appeared to have come through the mail.

"Present from a secret admirer?" Gibb joked, as Carlisle glanced toward him.

"Nope," said Carlisle as he stood up, "it's for you, 'Russell'."

Gibb grimaced. "Man, I hate that! Why does everyone insist on calling me that?" Gibb walked over to the package and tried to pick it up. It was too heavy, so he pulled the letter addressed to 'Russell' off the box.

"It's from Capitol Records," Gibb read out. "What in the world could they want?"

Carlisle shrugged as Gibb tore into the envelope. He chuckled as he read the letter to himself and then he passed it to his comrade.

"They sent me a copy of the entire Beatles catalog," Gibb revealed, "fourteen albums in all, to thank me for my part in the rumor." Gibb chuckled again. "Christ, can you believe it? Bhaskar Menon, the president of Capitol Records, is thanking me for making them millions of dollars."

"Yeah," Carlisle said after reading the letter himself, "he says they sold a lot of records because of this."

"Is it any wonder?" Gibb smiled. "After all, you wear 'em out pretty fast when you try to play 'em backwards..."

* * * * * * * * * *

The University of Michigan campus was nearly deserted, as it was the Wednesday before Thanksgiving break. In the bleak morning light, a few hundred students traversed the dew-moistened grounds to attend their last classes of the week and

147

wish their friends a festive holiday. Among the stragglers on campus were Fred LaBour and his buddy Jay Cassidy.

"You know, by the time we come back to classes on Monday, the whole 'Paul-is-Dead' hoax'll be over," Fred remarked, betraying a certain sadness in his voice.

Jay nodded. "Yeah, the thing has died. No one talks about it in my Econ class anymore."

"But it was...uh...interesting while it lasted."

Slapping his friend on the back, Jay smiled. "*You* made it happen, LaBour. You're the king of the cluesters. You'll never forget what happened, and you'll never be forgotten!"

As the two young men approached the undergraduate library, Fred let a sly grin creep across his face. "I didn't start the death rumor," he snickered, "but I sure gave it life, didn't I?"

Upon entering the main reading room of the library, Fred felt the early morning cup of coffee begin to work on his bladder. He tossed his books onto a vacant table and headed to the restroom. All of the stalls were empty, so he darted into the first one in his path. As he turned around to shut the door, he saw the graffiti and couldn't help but laugh. His laughter reverberated throughout the bathroom. It was just too perfect. The graffiti summed it all up in four short words.

It said: "Fred LaBour is dead."

Addendum

"Ringo, Paul, George And John
Played A Trick And Put Us On;
Dropped Hints Paul Was Dead As Nails—
And Rocketed Their Record Sales!"
—*Mad Magazine* (December 1969)

The quotations above and below have been drawn from the popular American electronic, print and other media of the past twenty-four years, and illustrate the extent to which the "Paul-is-Dead" hoax and the fallout from it has become part of our collective cultural memories.

ANGEL I: Is there any truth to the rumor that Paul McCartney is still alive?
ANGEL II: I doubt it. Where do you think we get these groovy harp arrangements?
—"Rowan and Martin's Laugh-In" (February 23, 1970)

[Sound of car crash]
ANNOUNCER: Clue number two...
BRITISH VOICE: Paul's been slain in a bloody car crash.
—Found between the grooves on **National Lampoon's Radio Dinner** (Blue Thumb Records, 1972)

SOME PEOPLE WANT TO RID THE WORLD
  OF PAUL McCARTNEY;
WHAT'S WRONG WITH THAT,
  I'D LIKE TO KNOW...
—The Swinging Erudites, sung to the tune of "Silly Love Songs" (One-Dimensional Records, 1988)

LENNON'S STAR VANDALIZED: Workmen yesterday repaired John Lennon's Hollywood Walk of Fame star, which had been vandalized and marred with "I buried John" scrawled above the slain musician's name.

The words "I buried John" echo those that some Beatles fans claim to hear in the group's song "Strawberry Fields Forever."

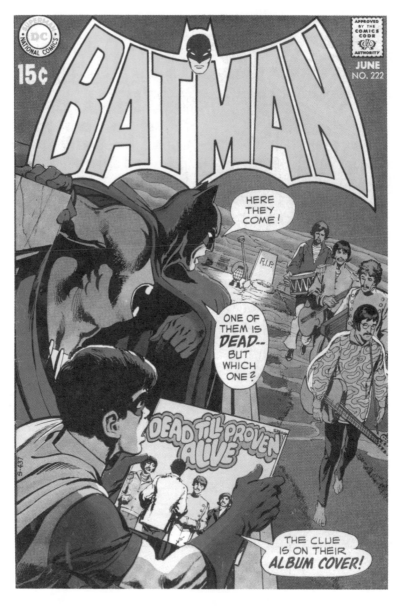

BATMAN AND ROBIN IN "DEAD 'TIL PROVEN ALIVE!"
The "Caped Crusader" confronts the mystery of the 'death' of
Saul Cartwright of the "Oliver Twists" in the June 1970 issue (No.222) of
Batman comics—only to find that it was actually Glennan, Hal, and Benji, the
three other "Twists," who had been killed in a plane crash in the Himalayas.
(Photo from the author's collection.)

Many believe the words "I buried Paul" are heard at the end of the song—claims that sparked rumors among Beatle devotees during the late 1960s that Paul McCartney was dead and another musician had taken his place in the fabled band.

The damage to the star was repaired early yesterday...tomorrow's unveiling ceremony [will] take place on schedule, with Lennon's widow Yoko Ono in attendance.

—From UPI (September 28, 1988)

Rumors that Elvis Costello had died circulated around Los Angeles in late August, the result of a hoax perpetrated by two DJs on the new music station KROQ-FM. The DJs, discussion reports of Elvis Presley sightings around the country, said, "Elvis is dead," on the air and then played a Costello song, continuing the stunt for several days. Costello's record company, Warner Bros., was besieged with calls from fans, and Costello himself phoned the label's president to assure him that he was indeed alive.

—From *Rolling Stone* (October 20, 1988)

CHRIS: You remember when you were with the Beatles, and you were supposed to be dead? And...uh...there was all these clues, that...like...you play some song backwards and it'd say...like...'Paul is dead.' And...uh...everyone thought you were dead...or somethin'....

PAUL: Yeah.

CHRIS: Uh, that was a hoax, right?

PAUL: Yeah, I wasn't really dead.

CHRIS: Right.

—From an "interview" with Paul McCartney on the "Chris Farley Show" segment of "Saturday Night Live" (February 13, 1993)

KID: Hey, Dad, did you know if you play this record backwards, it says 'Paul is Dead'?

DAD (played by Tom Hanks, standing at his son's bedroom doorway): Yeah, I knew that.

—From the film "Sleepless In Seattle" (1993)

151

SGT. PEPPER BOOTLEG ALBUM JACKET
An outtake from the Sgt. Pepper photo session.
(Photo by Michael Cooper, from the author's collection.)

Appendix I.
"...Here's Another Clue For You All..."

No compendium of clues could ever hope to call itself complete, but what follows are seventy of the clues that the kids found during the fall of 1969. The evidence is of both a visible and audible nature. A comment follows most of the entries.

Sgt. Pepper's Lonely Hearts Club Band (Album cover)

1. There appears to be a burial scene in the foreground, with either: (a) a left-handed bass guitar, (b) the letter "P," or (c) the word "PAUL?"
COMMENT: Peter Blake, the album sleeve's designer, relates that a young boy was helping to lay out the floral arrangements and asked him if he could make a guitar out of hyacinths. Blake found it to be a "sweet" idea and consented.

2. On the lap of the doll on the right-hand side of the cover, a toy Aston-Martin is either in flames or filled with blood. This is a model of the car in which Paul McCartney allegedly perished on November 9, 1966.
COMMENT: Eye of the beholder.

3. The rest of the Beatles have their bodies turned toward Paul, as if they were propping him up.
COMMENT: There are numerous outtakes of this photo with the Beatles in a variety of poses. It is pure coincidence (or a matter of aesthetics) that this one was used.

4. The wax effigy of Paul appears to be staring at the bass drum. If one takes a small mirror and splits the words "LONELY HEARTS" in half with the mirror at a right angle to the cover, there is a secret message: "ONE HE DIE."
COMMENT: It doesn't read like that at all. What it says is: "IONEIX HE♦DIƐ." However, if you still see the cryptic phrase among the letters, all you need to do to find a dead Beatle is locate the third face down from the left corner of the cover. It's

DETAIL FOR CLUE #2.

DETAIL FOR CLUE #4.

DETAIL FOR CLUE #5.

DETAIL FOR CLUE #6.

DETAIL FOR CLUE #7.

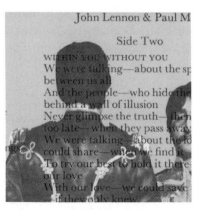

DETAIL FOR CLUES #8 & #9.

the face of Stuart Sutcliffe, the former bassist. He died tragically in 1962.

5. Paul has an open-palmed hand raised above his head. This is an Eastern symbol of divine blessing for someone about to receive a religious burial.
COMMENT: See Clue #3 and Clues #28, 31 and 52.

6. Inside the cover, Paul is wearing an arm-patch which reads: "O.P.D."; this stands for "Officially Pronounced Dead," the British equivalent of "Dead On Arrival."
COMMENT: There is a wrinkle in the patch. The letters *really* read: "O.P.P." and the patch is the official one worn by the Ontario Provincial Police. (Ironically, this fact was known at the time of the rumor by some of the Canadian radio stations, but it did not receive wide coverage.)

7. Paul is wearing the British Medal of Valor for dying a heroic death.
COMMENT: It is not a Medal of Valor. Besides, George Harrison is wearing the same medal—does that mean he's dead, too?

8. On the back cover, Paul is the only Beatle with his back turned toward the camera.
COMMENT: A matter of interpretation. Some said this didn't mean he was dead, but that he was being "singled out." McCartney told *Musician* magazine in 1980 that, "it was just a goof when we were doing the photos. I turned my back and it was just a joke."

9. The words "without you" appear beside Paul's head.
COMMENT: Coincidence. It's also a coincidence that the words "Nothing to do to save his life" appear above Ringo's head.

Sgt. Pepper's Lonely Hearts Club Band (Lyrics)

10. In the title song, we are introduced to a character

155

named "Billy Shears." This is the "double" who took McCartney's place in the band after the accident. It is probably a nickname for William Campbell, the winner of the Paul look-alike contest held in Britain in 1967.

COMMENT: As pointed out in the text (see Chapter XI), James Barry Keefer (Keith, of "98.6" fame) was the contest winner. "William Campbell" was a name made up by Fred LaBour for his *Michigan Daily* article. As far as the identity of "Billy Shears"—Ringo Starr, not Paul, sings the song attributed to Billy. "Ringo's Billy Shears," McCartney has said, "He always has been and always will be."

11. "Fixing A Hole" is about tending to an injury in the head, where someone's mind is wandering. Is that someone Paul?

COMMENT: A matter of interpretation.

12. In "She's Leaving Home," two times are mentioned: Wednesday morning at five o'clock and Friday morning at nine o'clock. If a secret phone number (probably the one from the **Magical Mystery Tour** cover; see Clue #19) is dialed at one of these times, the caller will make contact with Billy Shears or William Campbell. If they can answer some questions pertaining to certain clues, then they will receive tickets to Pepperland or a secret Beatles island.

COMMENT: As explained in the text, this clue sparked a rumor within the rumor. The *Washington Evening Star* (October 25, 1969) reported on a story that was floating around: "A student from Northwestern U. [called the number] and he was asked questions and when he answered them all correctly, he was invited to Pepperland. Seven days later he received an envelope in the mail with an invitation and tickets to Pepperland. The invitation instructed the student to lick the stamp, after which he became very apathetic and dropped out of school. Shortly after this, he told his friends he was going to Pepperland and jumped out a fifth-story window."

All of this shows the extent to which the cluesters would go to find an answer to the mystery. Additionally, it demonstrates how the rumor fed upon itself through the abundance of media coverage. The more the rumor was mentioned in print, the more it was accepted and talked about; the more it was talked about, the more press it received.

13. "Within You, Without You" talks about being unable to find the truth until it's too late "when they pass away." Life goes on "without you." Without Paul?

COMMENT: Selectively choosing phrases from George Harrison's ode to Eastern philosophy will get a person any meaning they conveniently seek.

14. In "Lovely Rita," there is the line "Took her home, I nearly made it." Paul and the meter maid perished together in his Aston-Martin.

COMMENT: Taken in context, the phrase obviously alludes to sex, not death.

15. In "Good Morning, Good Morning," John Lennon laments, "Nothing to do to save his life..."

COMMENT: It is fascinating that death is often mentioned in Beatles lyrics. Even as far back as 1965, songs like "Run For Your Life" and "In My Life" contained lyrical references to death—however tongue-in-cheek they may have been. "Good Morning, Good Morning" is another one of Lennon's imagery songs; he used strange words and phrases to evoke a mental picture for the listener.

16. On mono pressings of the album, a voice can be heard shouting under the music of the title song's reprise. The voice is shouting, "Paul McCartney is dead, everybody! Really, really dead!"

COMMENT: Before the **Abbey Road** album, producer George Martin prepared separate mono mixes of an LP, instead of simply combining both the channels of the stereo mix. This would occasionally result in two very different mixes of the same song. In this case, the "Sgt. Pepper's Reprise" does contain some shouting that is not as evident in the stereo mix. What is being said, however, is difficult to discern (Note: The mono version of the album is still available as a Japanese import.]

17. "A Day In the Life" mentions a man who "blew his mind out in a car." Along with other references to car crashes in various Beatles songs, this describes McCartney's death.

COMMENT: John Lennon and other Beatles associates have maintained that the reference is about Tara Brown, heir to the Guinness Brewery fortune, who met his fate in an auto accident in 1966.

18. On European pressings of the album, there is an inner groove after "A Day In the Life" which contains :02 of chattering. When played forward and backward, various messages can be heard. One voice says: "Paul's found heaven."

COMMENT: In Mark Lewisohn's excellently-researched work, *The Beatles: Recording Sessions*, the April 21, 1967 session for the inner groove is described in detail. Explains recording engineer Geoff Emerick: "They made funny noises, said random things; just nonsense."

When the segment is played backwards, one phrase comes through loud and clear: "We'll all be back here soon, till then, goodbye."

Hardly the stuff of death rumors.

Magical Mystery Tour (Album cover/booklet)

19. The name "BEATLES" appears in a pattern of stars on the front sleeve. If read upside-down, the word becomes a series of numbers—a phone number: 537-1038. If this number is called at a certain time (see Clue #12], one can speak to Billy Shears or William Campbell.

COMMENT: A matter of interpretation and an active imagination.

20. The Beatles are dressed in various animal costumes. Paul is the Walrus, which is a symbol of death in some Scandinavian cultures. The word is also translated in Greek as "corpse."

Magical Mystery Tour (LP)

COMMENT: Go to a large library and do some research. The assertions are nonsense. (Walrus is derived from the Dutch phrase, "whale-horse").

21. On the inside of the album gatefold, there is a twenty-four-page souvenir booklet containing photographs from the film. Beginning on page 2, and occurring several times in the booklet, we see an unfamiliar man in a bowler hat seated near Paul. This is William Campbell/Billy Shears.
COMMENT: Since the movie was not shown in America (except in very limited theatrical release) in the sixties, the cluesters did not realize that the man in the bowler is Mal Evans, Beatles roadie and confidant.

22. On page 3, Paul is seated at a desk behind a sign that reads: "I WAS" or "I YOU WAS."
COMMENT: "I YOU WAS," which is how the sign literally reads, sounds like a Lennonism very similar to "I am he as you are he..." from his song, "I Am the Walrus."

23. On page 6, there is a sign that reads, "The best way to go is by M&D Co." M&D Co. is a funeral parlour in Great Britain.
COMMENT: No such organization existed in Great Britain between 1966-69.

24. On page 9, the second panel of a cartoon shows a drawing of Paul with his eyes closed. His head is split open by the letter "L" in the lettering.
COMMENT: Eye of the beholder.

25. Also on page 9, in the text of the last panel, there is the following exchange: "'I Am the Walrus,' says John. 'No, You're Not,' cries Nicola." In the song listing on the inside front cover, a similar phrase appears. If John is not the Walrus, then it must be Paul (see also Clue #44].

26. On page 13, there are a pair of shoes next to the

DETAIL FOR CLUE #21.

DETAIL FOR CLUE #23.

DETAIL FOR CLUE #24.

DETAIL FOR CLUE #27.

DETAIL FOR CLUE #28.

DETAIL FOR CLUE #30.

drums. They are blood-stained. Paul is barefoot.

27. On page 15, there is a drawing of Paul playing with a toy car. Once again, his eyes are closed.

28. On page 18, there is a hand over Paul's head again (see Clues #5, #31 and #52].

29. On page 21, in the upper right-hand corner, an automobile accident is about to occur.
COMMENT: If the accident hasn't occurred, how can we be sure that it will?

30. On page 23, the Beatles are all in tuxedos. Only Paul has a black carnation on his lapel. The others have red ones. Black flowers are rare and considered unlucky.
COMMENT: If we are to believe Paul, he has maintained for the past twenty years that the costumers simply ran out of red carnations. Other people from the film production support this.

31. On page 24, the man in the bowler hat has his hand over Paul's head (see Clue #21 and Clues #5, #28 and #52).

Magical Mystery Tour (Lyrics)

32. In the title song, the Magical Mystery Tour that is being referred to is death. In fact, the Tour is "dying to take you away."
COMMENT: A matter of interpretation.

33. In "The Fool On the Hill," Paul is singing about a corpse—"The man with the foolish grin is keeping perfectly still."
COMMENT: One of the characteristics of the rumor was the way *any* phrase could be taken out of context and applied to the theory.

34. If the entire song, "Your Mother Should Know" is played backwards, it will reveal phrases such as: "why doesn't she know me dead," "I shed the light," and "why doesn't she ask my mind to be sure."

COMMENT: This is the clue that spooked WKNR disk jockey Russ Gibb (see Chapter X). When a song with no intentional "backwards masking" is played in reverse, it can sound strange and other-worldly. Although the language becomes gibberish, one can sometimes hear what amounts to complete English phrases; it is entirely in the ear of the beholder. (Some U.S. Congressmen even like to play this game. Representative Robert K. Dornan of California once introduced a bill to label records that have apparent satanic messages. He claims "Stairway To Heaven" by Led Zeppelin contains the backwards phrase, "I live for Satan.")

35. "I Am the Walrus" is Lennon's tribute to his departed friend, Paul. "Stupid bloody Tuesday" is the day of the fatal car crash. The eggman is Humpty Dumpty, who cracked his head open (like Paul). The policemen in a row are the ones who were at the scene of the accident. The walrus is a symbol of death (see Clues #20, #25 and #44). John is "crying" over the loss of his friend.

COMMENT: John Lennon loved to paint pictures with words; to evoke odd images with his lyrics. He was inspired, in this case, by the books *Finnegans Wake* by James Joyce and *Through the Looking Glass* by Lewis Carroll.

36. In the same song, near the end, a radio play of Shakespeare's *The Tragedy of King Lear* can be heard. It is Act IV., Scene VI. It is a death scene and it contains the lines: "bury my body," "O, untimely death," and "what, is he dead?" This death scene is included in the song to tip off the public.

COMMENT: Mark Lewisohn recounts the September 29, 1967 session which resulted in the radio play's inclusion in "I Am the Walrus." It was pure chance—a live radio feed was mixed onto the master tape and the tuning dial happened upon the BBC's Third Programme where the play was being broadcast.

163

37. If the chorus of "I Am the Walrus" (i.e., the "got one, got one" segment) is played backwards, one can hear, "Ha Ha, Paul is dead."

COMMENT: ABC News presented this clue on national television. Although it sounds convincing, see Clue #34.

38. Near the very end of "Strawberry Fields Forever," John can be heard saying, "I buried Paul."

COMMENT: On various bootleg recordings of this song, the phrase is much clearer. What Lennon is really saying is "cranberry sauce." Both Lennon and McCartney have supported this in interviews.

The Beatles ["White Album"] (Album cover/inserts)

39. The cover is "mourning white."
COMMENT: A matter of interpretation.

40. On the photo insert of Paul, a deformity can clearly be seen on the left side of his lip. This person is McCartney's replacement.

COMMENT: Eye of the beholder.

41. There is a photo collage on the handout poster. One photo features what appears to be the decapitated head of Paul floating in a bathtub of water (or blood!).

COMMENT: Fred LaBour first "discovered" this clue and used a doctored version of the photo to illustrate his *Michigan Daily* article. The doctored photo was remembered more than the original one in the collage, which clearly shows Paul leaning back in a soapy bath. His head is safely attached.

42. In the same collage, there is a photo of Paul dancing. From behind him, a pair of skeleton hands are reaching out to grab him.

COMMENT: A matter of interpretation.

The Beatles ["White Album"] (Lyrics)

43. "Glass Onion" is British slang for casket handles. In the 1800s, caskets had round glass balls instead of metal handles.

COMMENT: Russ Gibb claims he found out this information after spending eight hours on the telephone. There is, however, no historical mention of such a device.

44. In "Glass Onion," John Lennon makes references to other Beatles songs. And he drops a bomb shell: "Well, here's another clue for you all/ The Walrus was Paul"! Along with the clues from MMT, this proves Paul was the Walrus—the symbol of death!

COMMENT: While it is true that Lennon makes a blatant statement about a "clue," it is not about Paul being dead. Said Lennon, in a September 1980 interview with *Playboy*: "Well, that was a joke. The line was put in partly because I was feeling guilty because I was with Yoko and I was leaving Paul. It's a very perverse way of saying to Paul, you know, 'Here, have this crumb, this illusion, this stroke, because I'm leaving'."

45. Ringo Starr laments the loss of his friend in "Don't Pass Me By": "You were in a car crash/And you lost your hair."

COMMENT: It is true enough that this song and "A Day In the Life" mention car crashes, but how can we be sure that these accidents involve Paul? A matter of interpretation.

46. At the end of "I'm So Tired," there is some mysterious mumbling. When this is played backwards, an eerie message is revealed: "Paul is a dead man. Miss him, miss him, miss him."

COMMENT: Although one might hear something which sounds like this in reverse, the mumbling is not backwards. Once again referring to Mark Lewisohn's *The Beatles: Recording Sessions*, Lennon actually muttered, "Monsieur, monsieur, how about another one?" (Note: Lewisohn had access to all of the original Beatles master tapes, so he was able to isolate incidences of curious speech).

47. When the chorus to "Ob-La-Di, Ob-La-Da" is played in reverse, it seems to say, "Ha ha ha, I know we did it." Did what? A successful cover-up?
COMMENT: See Clues #34 and #37.

48. At the end of "While My Guitar Gently Weeps," George Harrison wails, "Paul, Paul, Paul."
COMMENT: Ear of the beholder.

49. If the chanting of "Number nine" from "Revolution 9" is played in reverse, the voice becomes "turn me on, dead man"!
COMMENT: Certainly the eeriest "clue" to surface, it nonetheless must be a coincidence that a perfectly-clear phrase in the forward motion sounds like something else in the reverse motion. However, a deliberate phonetic reversal may be at work here (see Chapter IX).

50. "Revolution 9" is an account of Paul's death. There are the sounds of a car crash, screams, car horns, fire, and discussion about an accident and bodily injury. A voice says: "He hit a light pole and we better go to see a surgeon" and "My wings are broke and so is my hair."
COMMENT: "Revolution 9" was much the result of Lennon's relationship with Yoko Ono. It was their intention to produce an "accidental" composition; an aural equivalent of an abstract painting. To accomplish this, they constructed tape loops with pieces of random speech and sound effects and mixed them all live onto a master tape. Much of the speech is masked by backwards music and effects, so it is difficult to say for sure what is being said. Each listener hears something different.

51. "Savoy Truffle" contains the line, "When it becomes too much, you shout out loud." This is a description of Paul's felt pain.
COMMENT: A matter of interpretation.

Yellow Submarine (Album cover)

52. John is holding his hand over Paul's head (see Clues #5, #28 and #31).

COMMENT: The hands above Paul's head are all coincidental, but the cluesters needed a common denominator to explain them. Therefore, it was suggested (first by Fred LaBour) that it was a symbol of divine benediction. The explanation caught on and became accepted as fact.

Abbey Road (Album cover)

53. Paul is out of step.

54. Paul is barefoot—the way corpses are buried in Italy.

55. Paul's eyes are closed.

56. Paul, who is left-handed, has a cigarette in his right hand. It must be an imposter.

57. There is a Volkswagen "Beetle" in the photo with a license plate that reads "28IF," which means Beatle Paul would have been twenty-eight years old IF he had lived.

58. The procession across Abbey Road contains specific characters: John, dressed in white, is a priest; Ringo is smartly attired as an undertaker; Paul is the corpse; and George, in workman's blue jeans, is the gravedigger.

59. The front photograph was taken at the exact location of Paul's fatal auto accident. Paul died on Abbey Road.

COMMENT: The seven preceding clues all occur on the front cover. Let's debunk them.

Firstly, photographer Iain MacMillan took six shots of the Beatles crossing Abbey Road during the August 8, 1969 photo session. From the five outtakes (available in various publications), we see that Paul is wearing sandals in two of

ABBEY ROAD BOOTLEG ALBUM JACKET
An outtake from the Abbey Road photo session.
Note McCartney's sandals and lack of a cigarette.
(Photo by Iain MacMillian, from the author's collection.)

DETAIL FOR CLUE #54.

DETAIL FOR CLUE #55.

DETAIL FOR CLUE #56.

DETAIL FOR CLUE #57.

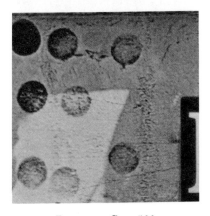

DETAIL FOR CLUE #60.

DETAIL FOR CLUE #61.

them. When the six pictures are all compared, it is easy to see why the one that was used was chosen -- it is the most symmetrical and pleasing of the batch.

Secondly, the VW "Beetle" holds no particular significance. Paul happened to be twenty-seven years old at the time, not twenty-eight. "It just happened to be standing there," explained MacMillan. "It had been left by someone on holiday—nobody with any connection with the Beatles—and a policeman tried to move it away for us, but he couldn't." (Note: The automobile fetched over $4,000 at a 1986 Sotheby's auction.)

Thirdly, the Beatles' attire happened to be what they liked to wear during the summer of 1969. Said Lennon during a 1969 WKNR interview: "They say I was wearing a white religious suit. I mean, did Humphrey Bogart wear a white religious suit? All I've got is a nice Humphrey Bogart suit. We all decided individually what to wear that day for the photograph."

60. On the back cover, there are a series of dots before the word "BEATLES." If the dots are connected with a magic marker, a message becomes clear: "3 BEATLES"!

COMMENT: Fred LaBour illustrated this clue on the F. Lee Bailey television show. It's true enough that a "3" can be formed by connecting the dots, but a "5" can also be brought out of the pattern.

61. Also on the back cover, there is a girl in a blue dress passing through the scene. If you look at the girl's elbow, you will see Paul's profile (his nose and open mouth).

COMMENT: Some people still see a naked woman on a pack of Camel cigarettes.

Abbey Road (Lyrics)

62. In "Come Together," Lennon sings "One and one and one is three." THREE Beatles?!?

63. In the same song: "He wear no shoeshine." Paul is barefoot on the album's front cover; he wouldn't need a shoeshine.

64. "Maxwell's Silver Hammer" alludes to death by a blow to the head.

65. "Octopus's Garden" is the British naval term for a sailor's final resting place after a burial at sea.

66. "You Never Give Me Your Money" contains the children's nursery rhyme, "All Good Children (Go To Heaven)."

67. "Golden Slumbers" is a reference to the Big Sleep—death.

68. "Carry That Weight" is a reference to the "Paul"-bearers carrying a coffin. It also refers to the burden the three remaining Beatles faced as they continued the group without Paul.

COMMENT: All of the lyrics from **Abbey Road** are a matter of interpretation. One remark should be made about Clue #65, however. It may very well be true that the British navy uses "Octopus's Garden" as a slang term for a watery grave, but no official documentation exists to back this assumption.

Other Sources

69. The bass-guitar style changed dramatically on Beatles albums after **Revolver**. This coincides with the date of Paul's "death."

COMMENT: The change in style of the bass-playing also coincides with a change in instruments. Paul retired his little Hofner violin bass in 1966, after the sessions for **Revolver**. "[Then] Rickenbacker gave me a new bass," McCartney told *Musician* magazine in 1988, "and I started to record with that. On the Pepper stuff I got into the more melodic bass lines."

70. On the sleeve for the Plastic Ono Band single, "Cold Turkey" (released in late 1969) there is an x-ray of a skull—Paul McCartney's skull after the accident!

COMMENT: It is actually a composite of two X-Rays—John Lennon's and Yoko Ono's—that we see on this now-rare sleeve.

Although most of the clues have been thoroughly debunked, you the reader may still believe that there is something to all of this. For you, an enlightening and entertaining thirty-page article by Joel Glazier is recommended reading. It first appeared in 1978 in the American fanzine *Strawberry Fields Forever* (issue #31). Copies are available from Joel himself. Contact:

JOEL GLAZIER
21 West 40th Street
Wilmington, DE 19802

One last clue needs to be presented—and it may say more than all of the rest. In 1971, John Lennon added the song "How Do You Sleep?" to his **Imagine** album. This acknowledged attack on Paul McCartney's integrity as a musician includes a very pointed line:

"Those freaks was right when they said you was dead..."
No Comment.

Appendix II.
"The Curious Case of the 'Death' Of Paul McCartney"
by Barbara Suczek

[Note: In 1972, less than three years after the "Paul-is-Dead" rumor made its appearance, University of California graduate student Barbara Suczek wrote the following article for the debut issue of a sociology journal entitled *Urban Life and Culture*. This fascinating study examines the rumor from a purely sociological angle and makes clear the inherent theological content.

After fourteen years as a lecturer in sociology at San Francisco State University, Suczek now works as a mediation counselor for Alameda County. She also belongs to a research team at the University of California that studies AIDS policy in the area of medical sociology and publishes the results in various books and articles.

Barbara Suczek continues to be intrigued by the power of the Fab Four—"It's amazing, isn't it? how alive the Beatles remain in people's memories."

With the kind permission of Barbara Suczek, then, we now present the "The Curious Case of the 'Death' of Paul McCartney."—**A.J.R.**]

It is a widely held notion that we are a disillusioned people living in a disenchanted age. Indeed, a belief that scientific advance inevitably leads to the demystification of the world—an eventuality that is sometimes celebrated and sometimes deplored—is so prevalent that it is virtually a modern axiom.

But to interpret *mystery* so passively—to think of it as being merely the effect of ignorance—is to neglect the implications of the active verb form: to mystify. Mystification does not, exclusively, *happen;* it can also be enacted. To mystify and to demystify are valid alternatives which humans can, if they choose, use in the pursuit of their individual or collective purposes.

An interesting example of the social construction of a mystery occurred in the late months of 1969, when a strange surge of excitement spread across the country, fomented, apparently, by persistent rumors relating to the nature and circumstances of the alleged death of Beatle Paul McCartney. By the end of October, the major news media were actively engaged in reporting the phenomenon.

Thus, a dispatch from Detroit appearing in the *San Francisco Chronicle* (October 23) stated, "The news director of radio station WKNR, which has been researching rumors and speculations about McCartney's death, said McCartney called to 'dispel rumors he might be dead.'"

The *New York Times* (November 2) said, "The half-belief in the rumor reached such proportions WMCA's Alex Bennett was sent to London to see if he could unearth some facts which might prove or dispel the stories. 'The only way McCartney is going to quell the rumors,' Bennett said, 'is by coming up with a set of fingerprints from a 1965 passport which can be compared to his present prints.'" *Life* (November 7) carried a statement from McCartney himself, in which he suggested, "Perhaps the rumor started because I haven't been much in the press lately."

Certainly the story had a strange quality about it; it seemed ghostly in sort as well as in content—the rumor of a rumor. Even the origin was obscure, tending itself to drift into rumor.

Whatever its source, the story spread widely and persistently. In New York, it was reported that "thousands of fans kept vigil at their radios" and that "mourners began appearing outside the McCartney home in London." The *San Francisco Chronicle* claimed that radio stations and newspapers were being deluged with calls asking, "Is Paul dead?" [1] Beatle publicist Derek Taylor was quoted late in November as saying that his Los Angeles office had received "letters and phone calls, day and night, nonstop since mid-October." A professor at the University of Miami reportedly "applied scientific voice detector tests to some Beatle records and concluded that three different voices are attributed to Paul McCartney." *Life* carried "The Case of the 'Missing' Beatle" as its cover story for November 7, presumably thus bringing the rumor to the attention of the remote outposts of the literate world.

The story, in gist, is as follows: Paul McCartney was

allegedly killed in an automobile accident in England in November 1966. The remaining Beatles, fearing that public reaction to the news would adversely affect the fortunes of the group, agreed among themselves to keep the matter a secret. Since it was obvious that Paul could not simply disappear from the midst without rousing a storm of embarrassing questions, they hit upon the idea of hiring a double to play his part in public,[2] a role that was filled to perfection by the winner of a Paul McCartney Look-Alike Contest, an orphan from Edinburgh named William Campbell. By an astonishing stroke of good luck, it turned out that Campbell not only bore a striking physical resemblance to McCartney, but was also endowed with similar musical abilities so that, with a bit of practice, he was able to sustain a performance that completely deceived an attentive and discriminating audience for almost three years. A slight awkwardness developed when a private affair intruded upon the public image: "Campbell" married the lady of his own choice, Linda Eastman, causing a short-lived flurry of consternation among Beatle fans who had for some time been expecting Paul to marry British actress Jane Asher. Miss Asher, the story goes, was paid a handsome sum to be quiet.

For some unspecified reason, however, and at some unspecified time, the plot seems to have undergone a qualitative change. "What began," according to the *Berkeley Tribe* (October 14-30), "for John Lennon as a scheme of deception conceived during moments of personal shock—and perhaps despair—developed into an all-encompassing religious vision."

Lennon's "all-encompassing religious vision," we are asked to believe, was oddly manifested by inserting cryptic messages relating to McCartney's death into the lyrics of songs and among the decorations on the Beatles' album covers.

The catalog of "buried" clues is lengthy and ingenious.[3] It includes such observations as the following: on the cover of **Magical Mystery Tour,** three Beatles are pictured wearing red carnations; McCartney's is black. On the centerfold of **Sgt. Pepper's Lonely Hearts Club Band**, McCartney is wearing an arm patch reading "O.P.D." which assertedly stands for "Officially Pronounced Dead" and is the British equivalent of

"DOA" (Dead On Arrival). In "I Am the Walrus," McCartney (or his reasonably accurate facsimile) sings, "I am he as you are me and I am the Walrus." The significance of this line is that "walrus" is supposed to be the Greek word for "corpse"--etymological authority not cited. (Webster says "walrus" is Scandinavian in origin.) If the song "Revolution 9" is played backwards, a voice (whose?) seems to say, "Turn me on, dead man!"

It is undoubtedly difficult for anyone not immediately caught up in the collective excitement generated by this macabre story to take seriously the symbols regarded as significant by those who were intensely involved in it. Nevertheless, for a period of several weeks[4] they *were* taken seriously and by a surprisingly diverse body of people.

Active rumor participants fell, basically, into three groups or publics: *believers*, who accepted the story at its face value; *skeptics*, who suspected it was a publicity plant to stimulate record sales; and *unbelievers*, who were convinced that the phenomenon was a manifestation of psychosocial pathology. Age was the most obvious variable separating the believers from the other two groups, believers being usually in the adolescent age range from about twelve to twenty. Older participants frequently seemed embarrassed by their own interest, tending to deprecate it even when the animation of their discussion seemed to belie the disclaimers.

Between and among the publics there developed considerable antagonism. It should be emphasized that, regardless of their credulity stance, all these groups were actively contributing to rumor process—the very act of opposition, irrespective of its direction, seeming to inflame tempers and produce rhetorical rejoinders. Rather than working together dialectically to create a consensual explanation for new and ambiguous events (a functional process theoretically attributed to rumor; Shibutani, 1966: 183), the publics in this instance seemed to withdraw into fixed camps, facing each other as factional forces dedicated to the defense of separate positions.

On the surface of it, it would seem reasonable to suppose that both the rumor and the factionalism centering around it might readily have been dispelled by the introduction of objective, reliable evidence confirming or refuting the fact of McCartney's death. The effect of the flow of information provided by the mass media, however, proved to be singularly unsuccessful in reducing public tension. Regardless of the play of coverage: "verified" facts, statements from McCartney, photographs of McCartney making the statements—the effect was to add fuel to the fire.

The stickler, apparently, is the matter of credulity: what evidence will be accepted as *reliable* evidence and by whom is not necessarily decided simply and objectively. Certainly the believers in the death story felt no lack of evidence in support of their belief. *Evidence* was the whole point! They were fortified, bulwarked, armed to the teeth with evidence; they had a veritable overkill of evidence.

The fact of the matter was that each public would accept as credible evidence only such data as suited the logic of its own cognitive system and thus it was that the more McCartney's death was denied, including by himself, the more the tension and hostility seemed to increase, feeding in and out of the interfactional dispute.

To account for the initial appearance of the rumor is, perhaps, the most perplexing aspect of the phenomenon. It seemed to emerge from out of nowhere, in response to nothing in particular and, as if at once to explain and justify its presence, the clues seemed similarly to emerge. But to realize the fact of the death depended upon recognizing the existence of the clues, and the clues were only recognizable if one were aware of the death. And so there is no external logic to guide a decision as to where the fundamental ambiguity lies—in the death or the clues—since it is impossible to establish a priority between them.

It *is* possible, retrospectively, to note changes in the behavior of the Beatles that may have contributed to public curiosity and speculation of the sort which—according to rationalistic, demystifying theories of rumor function—rumor is frequently addressed.

(1) Due to the increasing complexity of their music,

requiring the use of elaborate technical equipment and the manpower to manipulate it, the Beatles had reportedly been experiencing difficulty in presenting concerts that would satisfy the rising expectations of their record-listening public and, at the same time, uphold their image as a self-reliant, spontaneous group of four. For this reason, apparently, the number of their personal appearances had been decreasing.

(2) There were indications that the Beatles, as individuals, were growing weary of the limelight and developing correspondingly a taste for privacy and seclusion with the effect that, as in the previous case, they were becoming less visible to their fans.

(3) Paul McCartney had had a falling out with the other members of the group as the result of a dispute over management, as a consequence of which he had withdrawn from a number of Beatles' activities.

(4) McCartney had taken his fans by surprise by marrying Linda Eastman rather than, as had long been predicted, Jane Asher.

While these occurrences may very well have raised some questions among ardent Beatle fans, in and of themselves they do not appear to be sufficiently inexplicable or momentous to account for the fantastic content and public scope of the death rumor.

Clearly, the rumor's underlying logic is difficult to discern—so difficult, in fact, that—if logic can be said to exist at all--it appears that it must be sought outside the immediate subject of discourse. If this is the case, the rumor should be regarded as essentially symbolic, its characters and events standing for as yet unknown (and perhaps unknowable) social concerns. As such, its function is symptomatic; expressive rather than expository, problem-indicative rather than problem-solving.

The intriguing question inevitably poses itself as to why a group of young English pop singers should become the symbol for the expression of a social malaise. A clear answer is not easy to provide. It does seem reasonable to assume, however, that it is in some way related to the climate of intense excitement the group universally seemed to evoke.

The Beatles captured the public imagination almost from the beginning. Hunter Davies (1968: 179) says:

> Beatlemania descended on the British Isles in October, 1963, just as the Christine Keeler-Profumo scandal fizzed out. It didn't lift for three years, by which time it had spread and had covered the whole world...It is impossible to exaggerate Beatlemania because Beatlemania was in itself an exaggeration...It wasn't just teenagers; people of all ages and intellects had succumbed, though perhaps not all as hysterically as the teenagers.

Time (August 12, 1966) quoted John Lennon as saying that the Beatles were more popular than Jesus, an observation that occasioned cries of outrage but which may, for all that, have contained a grain of truth.[5]

The astonishing popularity of the group was probably due to a combination of factors, among them being the personal charm and youth of its principals, their exciting new music, and the phenomenon of mass communication. (The hysteria was unquestionably nurtured by publicity-conscious entrepreneurs.) When these elements came into contact with the Baby Boom generation—the largest group in the history of the world whose members were simultaneously in the period of adolescent identity differentiation—the effect was electric, in more ways than one.

Parents, educators, and clergymen viewed the phenomenon with alarm: the shaggy Beatle hairstyle looked bizarre to them and seemed to presage the ultimate collapse of middle-class values. The music sounded, if anything, more ominous than the hair looked, and the noise level achieved by the electronic instruments was predicted by "experts" to be a potential source of hearing loss and possible deafness. The, to say the least, *immoderate* behavior of some of the youthful fans in the presence of their idols was much publicized and completely unsettling to their elders. The John Birch Society was reported to regard the Beatles as part of an international Communist plot to demoralize American youth.

The more the older generation imprecated, the more cohesive in their devotion to the Beatles the youngsters seemed to become.

This is not intended to suggest that it was necessarily characteristic of adults to oppose the Beatles. On the contrary, there were many adults who were enthusiastic Beatle fans. There was, however, a marked tendency among adults—quite apart from whatever credulity stance they might individually assume in regard to the death rumor—to split into factions marked by opposing social and political values. Conservatives, for example, were much more likely to be negatively disposed toward the Beatles than were liberals.

It would be obviously absurd to argue that the Beatles—even had they been motivated to do so—could have produced this strange ferment of age partisanship cross-cut by political partisanship. Such a notion would surely exceed the fondest fantasy of the most ambitious public relations engineer! If the Beatles became the vehicle for the expression of preexisting social divisions (as they apparently did), it is probably due to a series of historical coincidences, not the least of which being the same sort of interesting propinquity that moved Hilary to climb Everest: they were conspicuously and invitingly *there*!

The most striking characteristic of the McCartney phenomenon is probably its preoccupation with the covert. Whether emphasizing *concealment*—as in the idea that the rumor was covering a sales promotional gimmick—or *revelation*—that it stemmed from John Lennon's motivation to communicate "the truth"--the "hidden meaning" motif recurs thematically both in the content of the rumor and in the explanations put forth to account for it.

There are, in all likelihood, many and various reasons for a public fascination with the idea of the concealed. The death rumor may be, for example, an inconsequential but interesting expression of the ethos of the Freudian epoch: an essentially artistic creation indicating public awareness of the concept of the unconscious--a folk equivalent of Surrealism.

Again, the fact that many persons apparently resisted all reasonable explications offered in the mass media, preferring to accept interpretations stressing occultism and deceit, may point to a widespread lack of faith in the reliability of information received through formal channels of communication. It may indicate that the much-discussed "credibility gap" is taking its toll by developing publics increasingly inclined to turn to folk communicational resources.[6]

However, the strange content of the rumor and its obdurate quality—the previously discussed failure of its publics to interest themselves in reaching consensual explanation—both suggest that there is something more than a mistrust of news agencies involved in this instance.

Another possibility is that there is demonstrated here a process of ordering seemingly random and chaotic facts into a system of meaning, the sense of the covert being somehow related to an inherent significance which is assumed to *underlie* the events of the world.

The Beatles had, over the years, moved from the straightforward, comprehensible statements of the "I Want to Hold Your Hand"/"I Saw Her Standing There" period of 1963 to the confusing and seemingly unintegrated verbal streams that are characteristic of many of the 1967 songs: "Lucy in the Sky with Diamonds," for example, and "I Am the Walrus."[7]

The "absurdity" of the songs was reflected in the style of the album cover decorations, those of the later years being typically designed as collages of apparently unrelated and randomly selected items.

Randomness can create a fertile field for subjective interpretation: one man's nonsense is another's apocalypse. To avoid the terror stemming from idiosyncratic isolation, however, it is necessary to establish a social basis of confirmation—some criterion—that what one takes to be a meaning is accepted and shared by others. Some such meaning-establishing process seemed to be indicated by the behavior of the younger adolescents as they busily conferred with one another evaluating the orthodoxy of the existence and interpretation of specific "clues."

It may be that the McCartney rumor reflects a search for

meaning that runs much deeper than a seemingly frivolous preoccupation with pop song lyrics and album cover art would seem to suggest. In periods of social unrest and upheaval, when traditional sources of authority are being challenged and overthrown, there is always the danger that human institutions will dissolve into primal meaninglessness. We may, in our own society, be presently witnessing the proliferation of interest in such occult phenomena as the I-Ching, astrology, Eastern mysticism, drug revelations, and the like, manifestations of efforts to shore up crumbling meaning systems. Perhaps there is a search for a new basis of authority and understanding represented here that is as profound as, on the surface, it may appear ridiculous.

That this fascination with the mystic seems particularly prevalent among the young makes sense when explained in the theoretical terms of adolescent identity crisis. Since it is this age group that most typically lacks the integrated convictions that might help to sustain a sense of basic meaning in times of extreme and rapid change, these are logically the ones whose worlds are most vulnerable when established bases of authority are assaulted.

In the past, it has surely been the function of great religions to organize and sustain the meaning and values of a society, but ours is a secular age. Basic religious tenets have been increasingly challenged by science; basic religious values have been subordinated to marketplace competition. It is probably not strange, then, that many aspects of the McCartney death story suggest an abortive attempt to apotheosize Paul McCartney.[8]

There are five specific properties of the McCartney phenomenon that would seem to support a conjecture that a myth-, or legend-creating process was at work.

(1) The content was relatively stable[9], lacking the ongoing, developmental quality that usually characterizes a news story. Among its believers, the story was taught and learned, deviations from the theme were definitely discouraged, and the fundamental details were memorized like a litany.

(2) The story shared with the legend a quality of empirical irrelevance. To whom, after all, but a few academicians, does it matter if legendary heroes actually lived and did the deeds attributed to them? The significance of the story transcends the details of individual biography. The fact, or lack of it, of the death of Paul McCartney seemed similarly irrelevant to its publics. The inference, then, is that the Paul McCartney of this story was a symbol, a social construct that no longer required the facts of a personal existence to sustain it.

(3) An almost Gothic engrossment with death and the occult permeated virtually every aspect of the phenomenon-- twin themes that are fundamental to myth.[10]

(The above properties, taken together, seem to fall into a familiar and ancient pattern. One senses in their conjunction a curious mandate that something must be fulfilled, calling for the recapitulation of a legend.)

(4) The content of the story recalls the pattern that categorically defines a cyclical myth. The untimely death of a beautiful youth who is subsequently transformed into or revealed to be a god is a recurrent mythical theme and is presumed to reflect the cyclical process in nature. The legends of Osiris, Adonis, Dionysis, and Jesus have all conformed, in some major way, to this pattern. It may be that the McCartney rumor represents an aborted attempt to re-create such a myth. Perhaps in the present, as in the past, humans may be trying to make sense out of the apparent senselessness of their own deaths by suggesting, analogously, the possibility of reincarnation. Alternatively, such a myth may be a process whereby socially valued qualities of an exemplary youth can be abstracted into an idealized model and thus preserved from the eroding onslaughts of ongoing reality (a motivation described by Wallace Stevens as "nostalgia for perfection.")

Whatever the reason for the recurring beautiful-dead-youth theme, its resonance in the McCartney story was clearly discernible. An embarrassed but eerie longing for the story to be true—for Paul to be really dead—was repeatedly expressed, such expression being invariably accompanied by protestations of admiration or love for the singer.

> (5) Clearly the rumor had high entertainment value. Not only did it provide a fascination subject for conversation, but it also invoked-particularly among younger adolescents—a fearful, brooding, supernatural mood which they obviously found rather more enjoyable than otherwise.[11] The entertainment component is an important factor in the promulgation of a myth since the pleasure of its company makes its repetition a likelihood.[12]

While there is a tendency to assume that myths and legends are essentially relics left to us, more or less by accident, from a long-departed and unenlightened age, there are many indications that the myth-making process is socially vigorous in the modern era. The spectacular rise of Mormonism in the nineteenth century is a striking example both of latter-day myth-making and the organizing force for social action that can emanate from a sacred mystery (and the myth that symbolizes it). Mystery resulting from ignorance can pose a potential and serious threat to human survival; as such, it urges the pursuit of knowledge to dispel it. Mystery, on the other hand, can provide a basis for human meaning, its sacred (and secret) premises upholding the perception of reality. In its latter function, it can be created and preserved by social volition; it can be institutionalized into a religion.

There are several factors that might help to explain why Paul McCartney may have become the unwitting subject of a religious myth. In the first place, there is the underlying context of the ecstatic reaction, especially among the young, elicited by the Beatles and their music. There can be little doubt that rock groups produce an auditory, visual, and sexual stimulation that is particularly impelling because of the intense effects made possible by electronics—sound patterns heretofore impossible to produce and control—and mind-splitting amplification. Heightened psychophysical reactions thus induced are further augmented by the contagion of collective excitement sweeping through vast audiences—the very size of the audience having been itself made possible by electrically amplified sound.

Since religion and ecstatic reaction have never been far apart, such orgiastic response might very easily be transferred into religious ecstasy. Middle-class nervousness in the face of religious intensity is quite accountable among people for whom rationality in the social order is particularly valued. These are rarely the young and even more rarely, evidently, the contemporary American young. The irrationality of ecstatic response may be the factor that can best explain the previously noted antagonism expressed by conservative adults not only to the rumor but to the entire Beatlemania phenomenon.

The precipitating agent transforming collective excitement into religious response might, hypothetically, have been a fortuitous juxtaposition of ideas. There are always disconnected and intriguing bits of commonly available information floating about in segments of society without an organizing explanation to pull them together: data in search of a theory. Relevant to the McCartney case such items might range from the high drama of the deaths of the Kennedy brothers—never explained wholly to the satisfaction of the general public—through the rumor-productive, year-long hiatus of Bob Dylan following a serious motorcycle accident; the accidental death of singer Richard Farina just as his career was gaining momentum; a curious public awareness of the rarely discussed death of one of the original members of the Beatles; the group's venture into Indian mysticism in 1967; John Lennon's previously mentioned comment, irrevocably, perhaps, linking together the idea of the Beatles and Jesus.

The choice of McCartney as a specific focus of attention may rest on the situational ambiguities mentioned above in which he, probably because of the vagaries of personal temperament, seems to have been the key figure. Added to this is the apparently undeniable fact that McCartney was regarded by many as the most handsome and the most romantically appealing of the Beatles. This being the case, it seems quite probable that Paul would be the most likely member of the group to be cast in the role of ritual sacrificial victim. He might very well have been, for a month or so, a candidate for deification—saved this embarrassment in the end not so much by his own stubborn insistence on proclaiming himself to be alive as by the approach of the Christmas holidays. There, in a strange sort of way, but for the grace of God, went God.

The public stir attending the "death" of Paul McCartney was obviously an amusing but trivial social phenomenon: short-lived and probably inconsequential. That it should have spread as widely and as rapidly as it did, however, suggests that there are processes of social interaction at work that it might well behoove us to examine more carefully. However foolish its guise, the McCartney rumor clearly indicates that there is a potential for irrational belief and action—be it constructive or be it destructive to what or whose values—that is alive and well in the modern, industrialized, "enlightened" world.

Notes

1. A similar phenomenon was noted in the wake of the death of Franklin Roosevelt: "newspapers, radio stations, banks, and even corner drugstores were deluged with calls asking if it 'was true' that this, that, or the other person had died or had been killed in an accident." (Jacobson, 1948: 460). The "secretly dead" pattern has its "secretly alive" counterpart. Thus, according to Jacobson, Roosevelt "quite apparently died as a man dies from a cerebral hemorrhage. But, according to the echoes of rumor, Roosevelt is still alive, in a madhouse."

In the past few years, there has been a recurrent rumor that John F. Kennedy did not die in Dallas but that he is being concealed—disfigured and brain-damaged—in a military hospital "somewhere" in the United States.

2. The "double" theme is a recurring one. During World War II, it was circulated in the United States relative to Adolf Hitler. Recently, we have heard it asserted of Mao Tse-tung. Jacobson (1948) mentions it in connection with Napoleon Bonaparte.

3. From the *Rolling Stone* (January 7, 1971): *Interviewer*: Were any of those things really on the albums that

were said to be there? Clues? *John Lennon*: No. That was bullshit, the whole thing was made up...We did put in like 'tit, tit, tit' in 'Girl.'"

4. On the basis of a quick rundown of press reports, it can be roughly estimated that the period of intense public excitement, at least the period during which the news media were actively contributing to it, lasted for approximately two months, reaching a peak in early November. After the last week in November, interest seemed to peter out, the most likely explanation being that public interest had been diverted by the approach of the holiday season. There was a brief afterglow on February 23, 1970, in a TV skit on "Rowan and Martin's Laugh-In": "*Angel I*: Is there any truth to the rumor that Paul McCartney is still alive? *Angel II*: I doubt it. Where do you think we get these groovy harp arrangements?"

5. For example, the following is from an interview with a fourteen year-old high school freshman (male) in November 1969: "Well, I hate to say it, but Jesus doesn't turn me on like the Beatles do. I feel like a hypocrite, but I think John Lennon was right when he said that. I get turned on by our church group, though. Like when we sit around together and discuss Galatians and we're all together and you really turn on. Like you love everybody--feel close to everybody...The Beatles are good. They tell the truth. They believe in love and people. They're against hypocrisy. They turn you on!"

6. And, as Leonard Schatzman has pointed out to me, the reverse can also hold true: folk communicational processes can create their own credibility gap.

7. Davies (1968: 282) notes: "They have used drug slang in their songs, but not as much as people have said...They are amused by all the interpretations. John deliberately let all the verbal jokes and stream-of-consciousness stuff stay as they had come out of his head in "I Am the Walrus," knowing a lot of people would have fun trying to analyze them."

John Lennon (*Rolling Stone*, February 4, 1971) says: "'Lucy in the Sky with Diamonds'—I swear to God, or Mao, or to anybody you like, I had no idea spelled L.S.D.—I didn't look at the initials, I don't look...I mean, I never play things backwards."

8. The inherent religiosity of the rumor has been noted by a number of writers. For example, J Marks (*New York Times*, November 2, 1969): "The death and resurrection of heroes appears to be as important to the generation that worships rock as it is to the tribes that celebrate the demise and return of various vegetable gods. Whether the McCartney death is purely physical or metaphorical or even metaphysical, it is probable that there is more than a little of the mythic logic of the Cambridge school of classical anthropology involved in the Paul-Messiah myth."

Ralph J. Gleason (*San Francisco Examiner*, November 5, 1969): "They've got it all wrong. It's god that's dead, not Paul McCartney...No one believes in anything anymore and man has a deep need to believe. Remove his objects of belief and he will invent others."

John Lennon (*Rolling Stone*, January 7, 1971): "Whenever we went on tour in Britain and everywhere we went, there were always a few seats laid aside for cripples and people in wheelchairs...the mothers would push them at you like you were Christ or something, or as if there were some aura about you which would rub off on them...It seemed like we were just surrounded by cripples and blind people all the time, and when we would go through corridors, they would all be touching us and things like that. It was horrifying."

9. "Legends persist because...they provide answers to the persistent riddles of life or, with fine or only metaphoric precision, deep human feelings...Legends that deal with primal forces, cosmology, religious belief, are technically called *myths*...they are especially resistant to change." (Allport and Postman, 1967: 164).

10. "The roots of myth and ritual [go] down to the black subsoil of the grave-cult and the fear of death." (Max Muller in Campbell, 1969: 31).

11. Typical comments of thirteen and fourteen year-olds are the following: "It makes me all tingly!" "...dark! It's a very dark feeling. I don't know how else to tell you." "It's mysterious and creepy. Sometimes it's depressing." "You're hooked in to somethin—something strange!"

12. "[Myths] are religious recitations conceived as symbolic of the play of eternity in time...Myths and legends may furnish entertainment incidentally, but they are essentially tutorial." (Campbell, 1969:16).

References

Allport, G.V. and L. Postman (1967) *The Psychology of Rumor*. New York: Holt.

Campbell, J. (1969) *The Flight of the Wild Gander*. New York: Viking.

Davies, H. (1968) *The Beatles: The Authorized Biography*. New York: McGraw-Hill

Jacobson, D.J. (1948) *The Affairs of Dame Rumor*. New York: Rinehart.

Shibutani, T. (1966) *Improvised News*. Indianapolis: Bobbs--Merrill.

Appendix III.
Other Significant Rumors About The Beatles

LORD SITAR

In the summer of 1968, an interesting album was released by Capitol Records. The album, titled **Lord Sitar** (ST-2916) and credited to same, contained no information about the musicians who appeared on it. Since the recording consisted entirely of sitar instrumentals, it was immediately suggested by the press and fans alike that "Lord Sitar" was a George Harrison pseudonym. After all, it was common knowledge that Harrison was quite fond of the Indian instrument, having utilized it on a number of Beatles recordings. Despite the excitement generated, the mystery album was surprisingly not a big seller.

The identity of Lord Sitar and the story behind the recording have only recently come to light (no, it wasn't George Harrison). An obscure Englishman named Jim Sullivan filled the shoes of Lord Sitar. He and other session musicians put the album together in France in an attempt to cash in on the sitar craze. The recording was then licensed to EMI Pathé Marconi. In turn, EMI associates in the U.S. and Great Britain obtained the rights to release the album.

THE MASKED MARAUDERS

At around the same time the "Paul-is-Dead" rumor was making the rounds, the mystery of the Masked Marauders reared its head. It all started with a satirical review of a record that didn't even exist. The October 18, 1969 issue of *Rolling Stone* contained the fake review (written by a "T.M. Christian" —get it?) which suggested that the Marauders were a superstar aggregation of epic proportions: the Beatles, Mick Jagger and Bob Dylan. Despite the obviously humorous nature of the tale, intelligent and well-respected people such as Allen Klein (then business manager of both the Stones and Beatles) and Albert Grossman (Dylan's manager) called the *Rolling Stone* offices and asked about the record.

It was decided some money could be made if an actual

album could be produced. A relatively-unknown coalition called the Cleanliness and Godliness Skiffle Band were tapped to play the role of the Masked Marauders and an album was hastily assembled, following the guidelines laid out in the review. It was played strictly for laughs; our friend "T.M. Christian" was even on hand to provide the liner notes ("The session went quickly...seldom was more than one take needed to finish a given cut. Often it required less than that.").

Although the Marauders rendered some pretty decent Jagger and Dylan impersonations, the resulting album didn't live up to its grand reputation. The final cut, "Saturday Night At The Cow Palace," admits to the hoax and identifies the record for what it is: "SHIT!"

THE FUT

In mid-1970, as the Beatles partnership dissolved, a single by a group called Fut appeared on a small British label. The recording—"Have You Heard the Word?"—sounded a great deal like the Beatles, and a rumor soon circulated that the song was the result of the Beatles' final recording session.

The only problem with this theory is the Beatles never wrote or recorded such a song. Along with other reference works, Mark Lewisohn's invaluable tome, *The Beatles: Recording Sessions*, makes no mention of "Have You Heard the Word?" having been part of the Beatles' output. Still, it has appeared on a number of bootleg albums and has been advertised as a Great Missing Beatles Song.

Although no one has stepped forward to take credit for the song, Harry Castleman and Walter Podrazik (authors of many Beatles reference books, including *All Together Now*) think that they have ferreted out the truth. They surmise that Maurice Gibb of the Bee Gees and Steve Kipner of the Australian band Tin Tin were responsible for the recording. [For specific details, consult the introduction to *You Can't Do That* by Charles Reinhart (available from Popular Culture, Ink; P.O. Box 1839; Ann Arbor, MI 48106)].

KLAATU

In August of 1976, Capitol Records released the debut album by a Canadian group who called themselves Klaatu. The self-titled recording was largely ignored by radio stations and the record-buying public in the U.S., but sales were respectable at home. Then, people started asking questions...

As the record began to generate favorable critical acclaim in Canada near the end of 1976, reviewers noticed that there was absolutely no information about the members of the band. Frank Davies, president of Daffodil Records (the band's Canadian label), fielded dozens of phone calls from the music press, but he refused to reveal the identities of the participants. The band, Davies explained to the journalists, wished to remain anonymous and be judged by their music alone. Although this was an unusual approach in the promotion of a new group, little was made of the anonymity until an article appeared in *The Providence* [Rhode Island] *Journal.*

Steve Smith, twenty-six, was an editorial assistant at the newspaper and a former rock musician. He picked up the album on a lark and liked what he heard. It was "refreshing" and had a distinctly "Beatlish" feel to it. Like most musicians, Smith was a voracious reader of liner notes. However, when he consulted the cover for information on the band, he, like the rock critics before him, became curious over the lack of appellations. All of the songs were written by "Klaatu." The compositions were published by "Klaatoons, Inc." Smith wanted to know who this band was, so he followed the instincts of his Canadian counterparts and called Capitol Records for details. The label claimed that they were as much in the dark as Smith was. They had agreed to release the album in America without having ever met the band. Executives in Los Angeles were impressed by the merit of the debut album and had negotiated a deal through Frank Davies.

Smith became suspicious—why would a major label like Capitol put money behind an unknown artist? It was then that the thought occurred to him. Could this unknown band in fact be the reformed Beatles? Certain songs sounded very reminiscent of the **Abbey Road** era. The voices, particularly on "Calling Occupants of Interplanetary Craft," sounded a lot like Lennon and McCartney. Smith began to scrutinize every detail of the album cover and the songs and found more similarities. In the same vein as the "Paul-is-Dead" rumor, he began to list "clues" which pointed to a positive identification:

(1) Klaatu is a character from the 1951 sci-fi film "The Day the Earth Stood Still." The cover of Ringo Starr's **Goodnight Vienna** album features a still from that movie, with Ringo superimposed and playing the part of the space emissary.

(2) In the same movie, Klaatu is asked where he is from. "Venus and Mars" is his reply. Paul McCartney and Wings' 1974 release was entitled **Venus and Mars.**

(3) At the end of a 1976 concert in Boston, McCartney bid the crowd farewell by saying, "See you when the Earth stands still..."

(4) The inside cover of George Harrison's album **33 1/3** contains a drawing remarkably similar to the cover of **Klaatu** (a sun with a face).

(5) In John Lennon's **Walls and Bridges** LP, there is a booklet with this quote: "On the 29 August, 1974 at 9 o'clock I saw a U.F.O." Many of the songs from the **Klaatu** album deal with spaceships and close encounters with aliens.

(6) At the end of the Klaatu song "Sub Rosa Subway," there are repetitions of short, backwards speech. When the record is spun in reverse, the voice distinctly repeats, "It's us...it's us...it's us." The song also sounds as if it is being sung by Paul McCartney.

(7) The song "California Jam" ends with a very Beatlish "Yeah, yeah, yeah."

(8) "Dr. Marvello," with an obviously Lennonesque vocal, concludes with the line, "Although it sounds absurd, we're completely cured and now we're fine." Had the Beatles patched up their differences and returned to once again make music together?

Steve Smith eventually unearthed more than two dozen "clues" and became convinced that something was going on. All of the ex-Beatles could be linked to the recording and Klaatu did, after all, sound remarkably like the Fab Four.

Smith finally followed the trail to Frank Davies and asked him, pointblank, whether or not the Beatles were involved. At first, Davies said no, it wasn't the Beatles, but when pressed about the band's identity, Davies laughed and replied that "everything that is there, can and will be identified even without...the people being seen."

Smith discussed his suspicions with the editor of *The Providence Journal* and received permission to write an article about the mystery. "Could Klaatu Be Beatles? Mystery is a Magical Tour" appeared in the February 13, 1977, issue and it became the shot heard 'round the world. Response was immediate; a disc jockey on WDRC in Providence read the article and dug out the album from the station's library. After playing "Calling Occupants" without comment, the phone lines lit up. Scores of listeners wanted to know whether they were hearing a new Beatles song. Others wanted to know if it was a previously-unreleased recording.

Word got around quickly and, within two weeks, the "mystery album" was selling out faster than it could be pressed. All those affiliated with Klaatu continued to keep their mouths shut. "What happened was so far removed from what we anticipated," Frank Davies recently related to this author. "It was as much a shock to us as it was to the industry at the time. It is certainly true that Capitol did nothing to suppress the rumor that started circulating [but] I certainly don't blame Capitol for that, since it built on the anonymity that [Klaatu] had requested of them, but at the same time, made marketing sense, particularly as they were then able to attach that anonymity to a vehicle to sell the band's records."

So, the silence continued and sales of the album skyrocketed. By the beginning of April, 350,000 copies had been moved and **Klaatu** sat impressively at #54 on the *Billboard* Top Album chart. Capitol, Davies and, presumably, Klaatu couldn't be happier. Whatever the reason for the sales, at least Klaatu's music was being heard by the masses.

But all was not well. Dwight Douglas, program director of radio station WWDC in Washington, D.C., was irritated by what he saw as a hoax and decided to do something about it. He led a "research team" from his station to the nearby Copyright Office of the Commerce Department and dug into the files. By law, it was required that the songs be registered in the real names of the composers; pseudonyms and band names had to be cross-referenced. Douglas therefore discovered the true identities of Klaatu: John Woloschuk (alias L.M. Carpenter and Chip Dale), Cary Draper, David Long and Dino Tome. As stated in a little-known November 20, 1976, *Billboard* article, they were simply a group of unknown Toronto session men.

When the truth reached the media on April 17, the bubble burst. Sales of the Klaatu album dropped off to a trickle and the band was universally shunned.

"Unfortunately," Davies says many years after the event, "Dwight Douglas and the media decided to label the band as a hoax, so overlooking the great talent and quality that existed in these individuals and the recordings they made."

But was it a deliberate hoax on the part of the band?

"There was *never* any effort, conscious or unconscious, by the members of the band or myself to perpetrate any form of hoax," Davies emphatically states. "The band, from day one, were anxious to take a different route to success than everyone else in the music industry. [The anonymity] was done in an attempt to create something different in a 'hype-conscious' industry."

It is indeed a shame that Klaatu weren't widely recognized and accepted for their unique musical statement. The controversy did irreparable damage to the band's reputation and they broke up in 1981.

Steve Smith still considers Klaatu to be one of his favorite bands. Others have recently rediscovered the band and public demand saw to the reissue of that controversial first album on compact disc (this time with songwriting credits). All objectivity aside, this author highly recommends the recording. You won't find John, Paul, George and Ringo on it, but you won't be sorry!

Afterword
by Joel F. Glazier

[Joel Glazier, a teacher from Delaware, has lectured extensively on the "Paul-is-Dead" topic at Beatle conventions, high schools, and on radio programs around the world. Three times, he has been invited to address the Liverpool Beatles Convention on the topic, and has been a contributor to many Beatles fanzines since 1974.]

What do *you* believe? Do you *really* think Paul is dead?

This question not only plagued Fred LaBour, Russ Gibb, and John Summer in 1969, but continues to be asked today.

"I haven't really given it much thought—the clues and the theories behind the clues are here for your consideration." This is my reply to the most-often asked question after the slide/tape presentations I have given everywhere from Liverpool, England, to New Orleans, Louisiana.

As you have read, the main concentration of cluesters in 1969 were found on American college campuses. I was fortunate enough to be on such a campus and get caught up in the mystery that has plagued a generation. At my University of Delaware campus, the "Paul-is-Dead" controversy pushed aside less academic pursuits, and local radio fed our appetites for clues, rumors, and questions about the life and death of James Paul McCartney (18 total letters in his name—that's 9 times 2, and he was killed on November 9 according to "Revolution 9"!!!).

Like many of the characters you have read about in this book, I, too, found the 1969 rumor scary, credible, and intriguing. As a Beatles fan (I saw them in concert in 1966) and a social studies major in college (I now teach), the "Paul-is-Dead" story tapped my two main interests. I had not heard a good cover-up story since the JFK assassination in 1963, and now here was one involving the Beatles (William Campbell/Billy Shears wins a McCartney look-alike contest).

As the major media lost interest in the "Paul-is-Dead" story after its obligatory one-month coverage, the clues and story still fascinated me. When the Beatles—namely Paul—announced their break-up in April 1970, many thought interest in the group would die. After all, now the Beatles as a business entity no longer would be there to field questions about their music, finances, or lives. But, many of the death "clues" were not satisfactorily debunked (and they never did produce old Paul and new Paul fingerprints!).

As the Beatles continued in their solo endeavors, I continued my following of their various successes and my collecting of Beatles memorabilia, books, etc., continued along with solo "clues" about Paul. ("Those freaks was right when they said you was dead," sang John; "All things must pass away," wailed George.) In the real world, revelations about Charles Manson getting "clues" and instructions for murder from Beatles songs, and another political cover-up of the Watergate break-in led to lengthy media focus in an otherwise boring new decade. (I did manage to get to the 1971 Concert for Bangladesh and, among others, heard the Paul sound-alike band, Badfinger, perform.)

Similar Beatles fans kept in touch as Beatles fanzines started appearing. These fanzines helped develop networks of Beatles fans from around the world (and beyond), and the "Paul-is-Dead" chapter of Beatles history always provided provocative and emotional responses among fanzine readers and writers. The first convention of Beatles fans was held by *Strawberry Fields Forever* magazine in July 1974 in Boston, and collectors, fans, and experts converged for a weekend of trading, films, music, sharing, and talking and talking and talking.

As a result of these hours of sharing and talking, I was invited to share my collection of theories and "death clues" in a two-hour slide lecture at the 1976 Magical Mystery Tour Beatles fansconvention in Boston. Alongside Beatles ex-manager Alan Williams, the other guest speaker, I discussed many of the clues included in Appendix I of this book. I also shared with the 1000 or so Beatles fans in attendance two theories about these clues—one involving a possible CIA involvement in the death of Paul McCartney (wasn't that John and Yoko in the audience at the Watergate hearings in 1973 when CIA agents were being grilled on their clandestine activities?), and another theory involving a Satanic Fautian deal the Beatles made in order to achieve fame and success (luckily, no Manson followers were in the audience).

From the stunned silence of ex-manager Williams and the hour of provocative questions from Beatles fans, it was obvious the "Paul-is-Dead" mystery continued to capture the imagination of both older and newer followers of the group—more than six years after the major media put the rumor to rest.

Since that July 1976 presentation where 1200 Beatles fans gathered to celebrate the British music group (ironically, during the month of the USA's Bi-Centennial of its break with the British), the collection of audio and visual death clues has continued to grow from the "basic 70" included in Appendix I of this book. Every October, radio stations have continued to feature "Paul-is-Dead" shows commemorating the 1969 rumor. References to the clues show up in Beatle interviews, videos, and journals on sociology, music, popular culture, and, naturally, in Beatles fanzines from Holland to Brazil.

At one time, a university course on the Beatles was unthinkable, but now—over twenty years after "Sgt. Pepper taught the band to play" and after the break-up of the band—many colleges offer courses on the Beatles, and the "Paul-is-Dead" chapter in their career is often the most popular part of the curriculum.

Will there ever be an answer to the *hundreds* of clues which suggest that it is William Campbell—not Paul McCartney—who filled stadiums with fans to enjoy concerts in 1990? As John and Paul once sang, "There will be an answer, let it be, let it be."

Additional Reading

The Library of Congress in Washington, D.C. is the superlative source for any newspaper articles on the rumor. Additionally, most universities keep archives of their student publications. A letter or phone call should get you a copy for a nominal reproduction fee. Although all of the articles cited in the text and the bibliography are recommended, those immediately listed below provide a real flavor of the time:

Recommended Articles

Aronowitz, Alfred G. "Paul Carries On in Never-Say-Die Spirit," *New York Post* (October 25, 1969).
>   Aronowitz scolds America for being so gullible and also gets Ringo and George to add their two-cents worth.
Burks, John. "A Pile of Money on Paul's Death," *Rolling Stone* (November 29, 1969).
>   Classic in-depth coverage by *Rolling Stone*. In addition, Burks claims to have heard the rumor as far back as the fall of 1968, when a young man arrived at the magazine's office armed with "clues."
Cassidy, Sharon. "Was It McCartney's Voice? Prints May Tell the Truth," *Detroit News* (October 23, 1969).
>   An even more complete transcript of the phone call to WKNR, and even more speculation about voice print analysis.
Clark, Joel. "Union Grad Documents Beatle Death," *Grand Rapids Press* (October 25, 1969).
>   An interview with Fred LaBour, a former student of Union High School in Grand Rapids. LaBour claims that his *Michigan Daily* article is "on the level, man."
Connolly, Ray. "I Didn't Know I Was Dead—Beatle Paul," *London Evening Standard* (October 22, 1969).
>   Article in which Connolly (an Apple insider) claims that McCartney is alive: "I have this on very good authority—he told me himself."

Farmer, Hugh. ' ' 'Tell My Fans I'm Alive and Well!' says Paul McCartney," *The People* (October 26, 1969).

Reporter Hugh Farmer recounts his Saturday journey to the McCartneys' Scottish farm: "I had to walk ankle-deep in mud. Paul does not hide the fact he likes seclusion when he comes to High Park."

Gleason, Ralph J. "Secular 'Saints' and a New Mythology" (in "On The Town" column), *San Francisco Chronicle* (November 5, 1969).

Gleason blames society's need for faith as the cause of the rumor. "It's God that's dead, not Paul McCartney," he argues. He then goes on to make several excellent points in order to prove his thesis.

Gormley, Mike. "Terry Knight Refuses Apple But Still Comes Out on Top," *Detroit Free Press* (May 2, 1969).

Detroit's favorite son discusses his future in the music business, pre-Grand Funk Railroad. Intriguing documentation of Knight's visit with Paul McCartney in 1968 and a mention of his upcoming Capitol single "Saint Paul." This article and the single appeared five months before the rumor gained national prominence. Quite possibly an indication of the origin of the "Paul-is-Dead" rumor.

Harper, Tim. "Is Beatle Paul McCartney Dead?" *Drake Times-Delphic* (September 17, 1969).

Significant because it is the first newspaper article on the rumor, appearing a month before the controversy hit Detroit. Harper based the article on stories he heard from his friend Dartanyan Brown. Available from Drake University, Des Moines, Iowa.

"I'm Not Dead, Beatle Paul Tells His Father" (uncredited Reuters news wire story), *Liverpool Daily Post* (October 22, 1969).

McCartney's hometown newspaper reports that Paul had to call his father and warn him about the false rumor.

Kronholz, June. "Miami Teens Sure Paul Alive," *Miami Herald* (October 23, 1969).

Reporter Kronholz talks to several students at Miami Beach High School and comes away with just as many theories: McCartney became a Yogi; McCartney is in a hospital with drug-induced brain damage; McCartney quit the Beatles to secretly raise race horses with his father.

LaBour, Fred. "McCartney Dead; New Evidence Brought to Light," *Michigan Daily* (October 14, 1969).

The newspaper article based upon the October 12th WKNR radio show, LaBour took the clues he'd heard and wove them into an elaborate theological myth. Much of the world's subsequent conjecture can be traced directly to elements in this article. Available from the University of Michigan, Ann Arbor, MI.

Lang, Kathy. "McCartney is Dead," and "McCartney is NOT Dead" by Owen Finsden (Chicken Farm Critic), companion articles from the *Cincinnati Enquirer* (October 26, 1969).

Lang's article is a serious review of the clues and the McCartney denials, while Finsden's piece is a spoof, claiming that Paul faked his death in order to pursue his life's ambition—chicken farming ("I am the eggman...").

Linedecker, Cliff. "Beatle Still Alive, Jeane Dixon Says," *Philadelphia Inquirer* (October 25, 1969).

The famous seeress gazes into her crystal ball and declares that McCartney is not dead.

Marks, J "No, No, No, Paul McCartney is Not Dead," *New York Times* (November 2, 1969).

A significant and in-depth article written by a former business associate of Linda McCartney. Marks attempts to explain why he thinks the rumor started by comparing Paul to the mythical Greek god Adonis.

Morris, Julie. "Beatle (?) Voice: 'Paul is Alive'" and "The Beatle Paul Mystery—As Big As Rock Music Itself," *Detroit Free Press* (October 2 3, 1969).

Reports from the home of the rumor. Comments and background on Fred LaBour and Russ Gibb. Plus, a printed transcript of the phone call to WKNR and speculation as to whether voice prints could determine the identity of the caller.

Oberman, Mike. "Top Tunes" (weekly column), *Washington Evening Star* (October 23, 1969).

An overview of some of the major clues, along with an

eerie report on the rumor-within-the-rumor (was there a student at Northwestern University who found Pepperland through a LSD-laced stamp?).

"Of Rumor, Myth and a Beatle" (uncredited essay), *Time* (October 31, 1969).

Contains a good sociological discussion of rumor-mongering, along with a satirical AP news dispatch. Perfect Halloween reading.

Rice, Joan. "Area Teeners: Paul's Alive and Swinging," *Akron Beacon Journal* (October 23, 1969).

Another field report on the rumor's validity, from the point of view of several Ohio teenagers.

"Rumors of McCartney's Death Put Beaucoup Life Into 'Abbey Road' Sales," *Variety* (November 5, 1969).

The entertainment trade journal concluded that the rumor had a positive effect on album sales.

Other Articles Consulted

Abrams, Jim. "'Killer' of Beatle 'Confesses'," *Indianapolis News* (October 23, 1969).

"Alive" (from the "People In The News" column), *Des Moines Register* (October 25, 1969). AP news wire story.

"Apple Corps. Says Beatle is Alive, Well," *Topeka Daily Capital* (October 23, 1969). AP London news wire story.

"Beatle Death Cult is Growing," *Miami Herald* (October 22, 1969). AP news wire story.

"Beatle McCartney Protests Death Report," *Washington Evening Star* (October 22, 1969). AP London news wire story.

"Beatle McCartney's Mystery Deepening," *Las Vegas Sun* (October 24, 1969). UPI news wire story.

"Beatle Paul Dead?—No, Kin Insist," *Jacksonville (Florida) Times-Union* (October 2 2, 1969). AP news wire story.

"Beatle Paul McCartney Denies He is Dead—Rumor Resented," *Concord Monitor* (October 23, 1969). AP news wire story.

"Beatle Paul Really Alive, Says Apple," *Bangor Daily News* (October 23, 1969). AP London news wire story.

"Beatle Spokesman Calls Rumor of McCartney's Death 'Rubbish'," *New York Times* (October 22, 1969). AP London news wire story.

"Beatles' McCartney is Alive and Kicking," *Denver Post* (October 22, 1969). AP news wire story.

Bernstein, Michael. "McCartney Death Rumor Won't Die," *Washington Daily* (October 23, 1969).

Boyer, Brian. "Paul McCartney Dead? Campuses Swept by Beatle Rumor," *Chicago Sun-Times* (October 21, 1969).

Cauffiel, Lowell. "Pop Scholar," *Detroit Monthly* (September, 1988). An interview with Russ Gibb.

Cook, Bruce. "Around and Around Go the Rumors," *National Observer* (October 27, 1969).

Deacy, Jack. "Paul McCartney Insists He's Alive," *New York Daily News* (October 25, 1969).

"Dead Beatle Mania Mounts; Sick Singles Issued in America," *Melody Maker* (November 22, 1969).

"Dead or Alive? The Mystery of Beatle Paul McCartney, or Reading Between the Lines," *Washington Daily* (October 21, 1969). UPI news wire story.

"Death Cult Forming Over Beatle," *Arizona Republic* (October 22, 1969). UPI news wire story.

"Fans Dispute Claims by the 'Late' Beatle," *Los Angeles Times* (October 22, 1969). Reprint of B.J. Phillips article from the *Washington Post.*

Fischer, Neil. "Drake Sophomore Wanted Alive in 'Death' of Beatle," *Des Moines Register* (October 23, 1969).

"He's Not Dead, Beatle Says Spiritedly," *San Francisco Examiner* (October 22, 1969). AP London news wire story.

"He's the Joker, Says Peorian," *Chicago Sun-Times* (October 21, 1969).

"I Am Alive," *Sioux City Journal* (October 23, 1969). AP London news wire story.

"'If I Were Dead, I'd Be the Last to Know'," *Duluth News-Tribune* (October 23, 1969). AP London news wire story.

"I'm Alive and Well, Says McCartney," *Hartford Courant* (October 23, 1969). AP New York news wire story.

"Just a Joke—'I Started Paul Rumor,' Teener Says," *Akron Beacon Journal* (October 23, 1969). The "teener" in question is Tim Harper.

"Kerouac Dead; Beatle No (?)," *Anchorage Daily News* (October 23, 1969). AP news wire stories.

Key, Ivor and Judith Simons. "Beatle Paul Takes Call: 'Dead? No, Not At All'," *Boston Herald* (October 22, 1969).

"Kids' New Macabre Game: Is Paul McCartney Dead?" *Variety* (October 22, 1969).

Mannweiler, David. "Beatle Death Rumors Buried," *Indianapolis News* (October 25, 1969).

"McCartney 'Death' Gets Disk Coverage Dearth," *Billboard* (November 8, 1969).

"McCartney Not Dead After All," *New Orleans Times-Picayune* (October 23, 1969). AP news wire story.

Neary, John. "The Magical McCartney Mystery," *Life* (November 7, 1969).

    Notable for two reasons: (1) Although the magazine didn't appear on the newsstands until the final days of October, the interview with Paul McCartney was the first one conducted since the onset of the rumor, and (2) McCartney gives the first indication that the Beatles were on the verge of a break-up.

"Newsmakers" (column), *Newsweek* (November 3, 1969).

"One and One and One is Three?" *Rolling Stone* (November 15, 1969).

"OWU Quintet In Middle of Paul's Death Theories," *Delaware Gazette* (October 23, 1969).

"Paul McCartney Death is Denied—But Rumors of Beatle's Demise Persist in U.S.," *Baltimore Sun* (October 22, 1969). Reuters news wire story.

"Paul McCartney Denies He's Dead," *Cincinnati Enquirer* (October 24, 1969). AP Detroit news wire story.

"Paul McCartney Discussion: Life and Death Rumors" ("FM Highlights" column), *Detroit Free Press* (October 26, 1969). Announcement of WKNR radio special, and WXYZ "Paul-is-Dead" show.

Paul McCartney interview, from *Rolling Stone* (April 30, 1970).

"Paul McCartney Refutes Rumors of His Death," *Buffalo Evening News* (October 22, 1969). Reuters news wire story.

Phillips, B.J. "McCartney Death Cult Growing" *State Journal* (October 25, 1969). Reprint of *Washington Post* article.

Phillips, B.J. "McCartney 'Death' Rumors," *Washington Post* (October 22, 1969).

"Rumor Scotched! Beatle Talks on Radio!" *Detroit Free Press* (October 27, 1969). Excerpts from BBC Radio.

Scott, Jane. "Paul's Death 'Exaggerated'," *Cleveland Plain Dealer* (October 24, 1969).

"Special Merit Spotlight," *Billboard* (May 31, 1969). Mention of Terry Knight's single, "Saint Paul."

Tschappat, Michael. "Is Paul Dead?" *Ohio State Lantern* (October 22, 1969). Available from Ohio State University.

Ulvilden, Barb. "Something Wrong With McCartney? Clues Hint at Possible Beatle Death," *Northern Star* (September 23, 1969). Available from Northern Illinois University, DeKalb, Illinois.

"Was It Paul Who Called Detroit? McCartney Dead? Nay, Says Phoner" *Delaware Gazette* (October 23, 1969).

White, Timothy. "McCartney Gets Hungry Again," *Musician* (February, 1988).

Paul talks about the rumor (briefly) and why his bass-playing changed so dramatically with the **Sgt. Pepper** album.

"Yeuch!" (from "The Times Diary"), *London Times* (October 22, 1969).

Books & Scholarly Journals

Bird, Donald A., et. al. "Walrus is Greek For Corpse: Rumor and the Death of Paul McCartney," in *Journal of Popular Culture* (Popular Culture Association, 1976).

A scholarly and heavily-footnoted study of the rumor by a trio of professors from Central Michigan University. It benefits by observing the phenomenon through seven years of hindsight.

Brown, Peter and Steven Gaines. *The Love You Make* (McGraw-Hill, New York, 1983), pp. 372-4.

An account of McCartney's unusual reception of Dorothy

Bacon and the *Life* magazine photographers.

Brunvand, Jan Harold. *The Vanishing Hitchhiker: American Urban Legends And Their Meanings* (W.W. Norton & Company, New York, 1984).

> Nothing here as specific reference to the McCartney rumor, but an in-depth study on the spread of rumors in general.

DiLello, Richard. *The Longest Cocktail Party* (Popular Culture Ink., Ann Arbor, MI, 1983), pp. 213-5.

> An Apple Corps. insider discusses how the rumor affected the day-to-day operations of the Beatles' empire. Enlightening and humorous.

Flippo, Chet. *Yesterday: The Unauthorized Biography of Paul McCartney* (Doubleday, New York, 1988), pp. 298-300.

Herman, Gary. *Rock 'n' Roll Babylon* (Perigee Books, New York, 1982), pp. 147-8.

Lewisohn, Mark. *The Beatles: Recording Sessions* (Harmony Books, New York, 1989).

> An excellently-researched work that takes the reader day-by-day through all of the Beatles' studio sessions. Because of Lewisohn's access to the master tapes, he was able to debunk many of the myths about what was hidden on some of songs. Yes, Lennon *did* say "cranberry sauce," not "I buried Paul."

Marsh, Dave and Kevin Stein. *The Book of Rock Lists* (Dell/ Rolling Stone Press, New York, 1981), pp. 454-6.

> The authors list twenty-five of the death clues, some of them pre-Sgt.Pepper. True "cluesters" would say that such clues don't count as part of the evidence.

Morgan, Hal and Kerry Tucker. *More Rumor!* (Penguin Books, New York, 1988), pp. 84-5)

> A discussion about the minor resurgence of the "Paul-is-Dead" rumor that took place in 1980 when McCartney was busted for marijuana possession in Japan.

Morrow, Cousin Bruce and Laura Baudo. *Cousin Brucie! My Life in Rock 'n' Roll Radio* (William Morrow, New York, 1987), pp. 204-6.

> Cousin Brucie recounts his deejay life at WABC, includ-

ing the night when Roby Yonge was thrown off the air by management because he carried on about the rumor.

Podrazik, Walter J. and Harry Castleman. *All Together Now* (Popular Culture, Ink., Ann Arbor, MI, 1985), pp. 119-21.

Poundstone, William. "Secret Messages on Records" in the book *Big Secrets* (Wm. Morrow & Company, New York, 1983).

A lengthy discussion about "backwards masking" and several of the most famous examples, including seven Beatles songs.

Rosnow, Ralph L. and Gary Alan Fine. "The Paul McCartney Rumor" in *Rumor and Gossip: The Social Psychology of Hearsay* (Elsevier Scientific Publishing Company, New York, 1976).

Mixing sociology, psychology, and theology together, Rosnow and Fine attempt to explain why the "Paul-is-Dead" rumor was embraced by the culture of 1969.

Schaffner, Nicholas. *The Beatles Forever* (McGraw-Hill, New York, 1977), pp.127-9.

Sklar, Rick. *Rocking America* (St. Martin's Press, 1984), pp. 111-5, 141-6.

The former program director at WABC in New York recounts the night when he removed disc jockey Roby Yonge from the air because the jock ignored Sklar's directive that the "Paul-is-Dead" rumor was not to be discussed.

Suczek, Barbara. "The Curious Case of the 'Death' of Paul McCartney" in *Urban Life and Culture*, Volume 1, Number 1 (Sage Publications, Beverly Hills, CA, 1972).

Yet another study of the rumor in terms of sociological and theological impact. (A reprint of this article appears as Appendix II of this book.)

Taylor, Derek. *It Was Twenty Years Ago Today* (Simon & Schuster, Inc., New York, 1987), pp. 35-6.

The former Beatles press officer tells of the photo session for the *Sgt. Pepper's Lonely Hearts Club Band* album cover and includes several of the photo outtakes.

PAUL IS LIVE (LP)
The perfect ending.
Released even as this book goes to press, the title of Paul's latest album
—comprised of concert recordings from his latest tour—says it all.
In a parody of the **Abbey Road** jacket, the license plate of
the once ominous Volkswagen Beetle now reads "51 IS"
—Paul's age. No doubt about it: Paul Is Live.

General Index

A

ABC-TV 91, 93, 164
AP see also Associated Press
AP 37, 52, 94
Abbey Road (LP) 7, 12, 15, 17, 21, 22, 34, 35, 42, 43, 52, 57, 65, 71, 74, 75, 76, 90, 94, 103, 104, 108, 114, 124, 157, 167, 170, 171, 193
Ace 121
Akron Beacon Journal (newspaper) 104
All Shook Up (song) 128
All Together Now (book) 192
All You Need is Love (song) 20
Allison, Keith 51
Altamont 111
Amish, Jean-Patrick 89
Andersson, Colby 99, 100, 101
Apple Corps. 11, 45, 47, 66, 93, 96, 107
Apple Records 9, 107, 119, 142, 143
Armstrong, Neil 36
Aronowitz, Alfred 111
Ashe, Penelope 23
Asher, Jane 21, 175, 178
Asher, Peter 21, 74, 76, 77, 78
Associated Press see also AP
Associated Press 29

B

BBC 40, 123, 163
Back in the U.S.S.R. (song) 21
Backwards masking 41, 42
Bacon, Dorothy 96, 98
Badfinger (performance group) 9, 198
Bailey, F. Lee 55, 73, 74, 75, 76, 77, 78, 81, 170
The Ballad of Paul (song) 82, 88
Baltimore Orioles 99
Barrett, Ronnie 91
Batman (comic book) 150
"Bbig Ssur" 3
The Beach Boys (performance group) 105
The Beatle Plot (radio program) 135
Beatlemania 39
The Beatles (LP) 11, 18, 20, 21
Beatles Book Monthly (fanzine) 140
The Beatles Plot (radio program) 107
The Beatles: Recording Sessions (book) 158, 163, 165, 192
Beckett, Katey 136
Beckett, Sam 136
The Bee Gees (performance group) 192
Belknap, Raymond 127
Bennett, Alex 36, 37, 63, 119, 174
Berkeley Tribe (newspaper) 175
Better By You, Better Than Me (song) 127
Billboard (magazine) 87, 88, 104, 143, 144, 195, 196
Billy Shears & The All-Americans (performance group) 85
Birthday (song) 11
Blake, Peter 153
Blind Faith (performance group) 107
Blue Jay Way (song) 20
Bob Seger System (performance group) 55
Bogart, Humphrey 170
Bonaparte, Napoleon 186
Brewer, Don 46
Brother Paul (song) 85
Brown, Dartanyan 27, 28, 145
Brown, Tara 158
Burton Tower 34
Butcher cover 105

C

CBS Records 127, 131
CFNY-FM (Toronto) 135
CKLW-AM (Windsor, Ontario) 141
Caldwell, Louise Harrison 17
California Jam (song) 194
Calling Occupants of Interplanetary Craft (song) 194, 195
Cameo-Parkway Records 141
Campbell, Glenn 51
Campbell, William 18, 20, 21, 51, 156, 158, 160, 175, 197, 199
Campus Corner 15, 35

Candlestick Park 112
Cannon, Paul 73, 76
Capitol Records 9, 46, 90, 104, 105, 106, 142, 143, 147, 191, 193, 195
Carlisle, Dan 4, 47, 48, 49, 107, 108, 135, 147
Carpenter, L.M. 196
Carroll, Lewis 40, 163
Carry That Weight (song) 171
Cassidy, Jay 8, 34, 36, 55, 56, 148
Castleman, Harry 192
Catena, Rocco 104
Chancellor, John 94, 126
Chicago Sun-Times (newspaper) 91
Chicago Transit Authority (performance group) 27
The Chicago Tribune (newspaper) 92
Chico and the Man (TV program) 87
"The Chris Farley Show" 151
Christian, T.M. 191, 192
Cinema Guild (of the University of Michigan) 8
City University (New York) 62
Clapton, Eric 107
Clark, Joel 44
The Cleanliness and Godliness Skiffle Band (performance group) 192
Cleave, Maureen 113
Cleveland Plain Dealer (newspaper) 45
Clues Revisited Ten

Years Later (radio program) 134
Cocker, Joe 89
Cold Turkey (song) 171
Come and Get It (song) 9
Come Together (song) 57, 73, 90, 170
Connolly, Ray 92
Cook, Bruce 53
Costello, Elvis 151
Country Wide Publications 81
Cream (performance group) 46
Creedence Clearwater Revival (performance group) 55

D

Daffodil Records 193
Dale, Chip 196
Datebook (magazine) 113
Davies, Frank 193, 195, 196
Davies, Hunter 20, 179, 187
Davis, Alvin 60
A Day in the Life (song) 17, 19, 33, 39, 60, 158, 165
The Day the Earth Stood Still (motion picture) 194
Dean, James 45
Dear Prudence (song) 11, 21
Delaware (Ohio) Gazette (newspaper) 43, 126
Delta Lady (song) 89
Democratic convention, 1968 125
Denbloch, Marilyn 124
Des Moines, Iowa 27

Des Moines Register (newspaper) 91
Detroit Free Press (newspaper) 69
Detroit News (newspaper) 69
Disc (magazine) 12
Dixon, Jeane 56
Donahue, Tom 60
Don't Pass Me By (song) 7, 39, 165
Dornan, Rep. Robert K. 163
Douglas, Dwight 196
Douglas, Mike 115, 116
Dr. Marvello (song) 194
Drake Times-Delphic (newspaper) 28, 91
Drake University 27, 28, 91
Draper, Cary 196
Duophonic stereo 106
Dylan, Bob 1, 27, 46, 185, 191, 192

E

EMI Pathe Marconi 191
EMI Recording Studio 17
EMI Records 9, 191
Eastern Michigan University 1, 124
Eastman, Lee 12
Eastman, Linda 12, 52, 81, 92, 175, 178
Edinburgh, Scotland 18
Emerick, Geoff 158
Engineered reversal 41
Epstein, Brian 18, 114, 119
Evans, Mal 160

F

Farina, Richard 185
Farley, Chris 151

Farmer, Hugh   123, 124
Farner, Mark   46
Feliciano, Jose   13, 59, 87
Finnegans Wake (book)   163
Finster, Werbley   13, 59, 87
Fixing A Hole (song)   156
Fogerty, John   55
Fonda, Peter   39
The Fool on the Hill (song)   20, 162
Fuse (performance group)   27
The Fut (performance group)   192

G

Gavin, Bill   60
George Washington University   69
Gibb, Maurice   192
Gibb, Russ   1, 3, 4, 5, 7, 8, 14, 15, 27, 41, 46, 47, 48, 49, 51, 55, 66, 67, 68, 73, 75, 76, 91, 107, 108, 113, 125, 126, 129, 131, 135, 137, 141, 145, 147, 163, 165, 197
Ginny   73, 74
Girl (song)   187
Glass Onion (song)   43, 48, 103, 165
Glazier, Joel   172, 197
Gleason, Ralph J.   112, 188
Glenn, Christopher   62, 99, 100, 115, 116, 117
Golden Slumbers (song)   171
Good Morning, Good Morning (song)   25, 40, 157
Good Night (song)   22

Good Vibrations (song)   19
Goodnight Vienna (LP)   194
Gorman, John   115
Got to Get You Into My Life (song)   55
Grand Funk Railroad (performance group)   46, 47, 145
The Grand Rapids Press (newspaper)   44
The Grande Ballroom   46, 107, 141
Gray, John   15
Greensleeves (song)   20
Grossman, Albert   191
The Guardian (newspaper)   119, 134

H

Hanks, Tom   151
Happiness is a Warm Gun (song)   11
A Hard Day's Night (LP)   71
Harmony Ranch (TV program)   131
Harper, Tim   28, 91, 145
Harrison, George   18, 20, 22, 61, 77, 81, 140, 145, 155, 157, 166, 191, 194
Hatcher Library   17
Have You Heard the Word? (song)   192
Haycock, Professor Everett   25
Hey Jude   9, 69, 103, 146
Hitler, Adolf   186
Hoffman, Abbie   125
Hofstra University   37, 56, 100, 124, 134
Hoops, Ray   69

Hopkin, Mary   9
Hot Chocolate   9
How Do You Sleep? (song)   172
How Much More? (song)   141
Humpty Dumpty   40
Hurkos, Peter   13

I

I Am the Walrus (song)   20, 31, 40, 69, 94, 160, 163, 164, 176, 181
I Saw Her Standing There (song)   181
I Want to Hold Your Hand (song)   181
I Want You (She's So Heavy) (song)   22
I Who Have Nothing (song)   46, 141
I'm Only Sleeping (song)   41
I'm So Tired (song)   1, 11, 41, 42, 165
Imagine (song)   136
In My Life (song)   39, 91, 157
Is Paul McCartney Dead Society   37, 56, 124, 134

J

Jackson, Gregory   93, 94
Jagger, Mick   191, 192
Japan, drug bust   136
Jay, Tony   104
The Jazz Masters (performance group)   141
John Birch Society   179
Joyce, James   40, 163
Judas Priest (performance group)   126, 127, 128

K

KGBS-TV (Los Angeles) 91

KIMN-TV (Denver) 91

KLEO-AM (Wichita) 60

KLEO-TV (Wichita) 91

KQV-TV (Pittsburgh) 91

KROQ-FM (Los Angeles) 151

KSAN-FM (San Francisco) 60

Keefer, James Barry 51, 156

Keegan, Victor 119, 134

Keith 51, 156

Kennedy, John F. 31, 186

Kent State University 125

King, Ben E. 141

Kipner, Steve 192

Klaatu (performance group) 193, 194, 195, 196

Klein, Allen 12, 73, 78, 143, 191

Knapp, Richard Terrence 141

Knight, Terry 46, 47, 141, 142, 143, 144, 145, 146

L

LaBour, Fred 5, 7, 8, 13, 14, 15, 23, 24, 27, 31, 32, 33, 34, 35, 36, 44, 51, 55, 56, 61, 73, 74, 76, 91, 112, 131, 148, 156, 164, 167, 170, 197

LaBricque, Michael 104, 106

Lady Madonna (song) 21, 52, 103

Led Zeppelin (performance group) 163

Lee, Mike 91

Lennon, John 3, 5, 11, 12, 18, 19, 21, 22, 39, 40, 42, 43, 60, 70, 81, 90, 103, 108, 111, 113, 114, 131, 134, 136, 145, 149, 157, 163, 164, 165, 166, 167, 170, 172, 175, 179, 180, 185, 187, 188, 194, 198, 199

Let It Be (LP) 12

Let It Be (song) 146

Lewis, Bob 60

Lewisohn, Mark 158, 163, 165, 192

Library of Congress 146

Life (magazine) 56, 57, 58, 77, 96, 98, 100, 101, 103, 119, 123, 174

Linkletter, Art 13

Liverpool Daily Post (newspaper) 107

Lock, David 114

Lomax, Jackie 9

London Evening Standard (newspaper) 92, 113

London Express (newspaper) 119

Long, David 196

Lord Sitar (performance group) 191

Lovely Rita (song) 157

Lucy in the Sky With Diamonds (song) 146, 181, 187

M

M&D Co. 160

MGM Records 82

MacDougall, John 123

MacLen Music, Inc.

(publishing company) 145, 146

MacMillan, Iain 52, 167, 170

Mad (magazine) 149

The Magic Christian (motion picture) 63

Magical Mystery Tour (LP) 4, 8, 9, 14, 19, 20, 21, 42, 43, 57, 71, 90, 104, 116, 119, 120, 124, 134, 156, 158, 160, 162, 163, 164, 175

Magical Mystery Tour (song) 20, 162

Manson, Charles 125, 198

Marks, J 92, 188

Marsden, David 135

Martin, George 17, 18, 19, 157

The Masked Marauders (performance group) 191, 192

Maxwell's Silver Hammer (song) 9, 19, 22, 171

Mazner, Merrill 91

McCarthy, Sen. Joseph 111

McCartney, Heather 65, 93

McCartney, Linda 65, 93, 98, 123

McCartney, Mary 12, 65, 93, 98

McGear, Mike 51, 115, 116, 117

McGough, Roger 115, 117

McKenna, Kenneth 127

McNally, Rand 36

Mean Mr. Mustard (song) 22

Menon, Bhaskar 147
Mercury Records 51
Michigan Daily (newspaper) 7, 15, 17, 23, 24, 32, 33, 44, 61, 112, 156, 164
Michigan State University 68
The Mike Douglas Show (TV program) 115
Milgrum, Stanley 62
Modern Jazz Quartet 9
Moratorium Day 33, 34, 37
Morris, George Taylor 136
Mr. Ponytail 70, 71
Musician (magazine) 155, 171
The Mystery Tour (performance group) 82

N
NBC-TV 94, 126, 136
Naked Came the Stranger (book) 23
National Lampoon's Radio Dinner (LP) 149
National Observer (newspaper) 53
Neary, John 56, 57, 58, 100
New York Mets 99
New York Post (newspaper) 111, 140
New York Times (newspaper) 92, 119, 174, 188
New York University 99
Newberry, Jonathan 23, 24, 33, 34
Newman, Bill 27
Newsday (newspaper) 23
Newton, Sir Isaac 142, 143
Nichol, Jimmy 65
Nickloff, William Jr. 127
98.6 (song) 51, 156
Nixon, President Richard M. 13, 93, 125
Northern Illinois University 28
Northern Star (newspaper) 28
Northwestern University 120, 156
Nurk Twins (performance group) 21
Nye, Philip 66, 67, 68

O
O.P.D. 19, 57, 107, 117, 124, 135, 155, 175
O.P.P. (Ontario Provincial Police) 135, 136
Oberman, Mike 120
Ob-La-Di, Ob-La-Da (song) 166
Octopus's Garden (song) 22, 171
Oh! Darling (song) 52
Ohio State Lantern (newspaper) 103, 126
Ohio State University 65
Ohio Wesleyan University 24, 25, 28, 121, 131
Ono, Yoko 3, 11, 151, 166, 172, 198
Oxford University 48

P
Paperback Writer (song) 146
Parlophone/EMI Records 105
Paul McCartney and

Wings (performance group) 194
Paul McCartney Dead—The Great Hoax (magazine) 81, 82
Paul McCartney: The Complete Story, Told For the First and Last Time (TV program) 55, 75
Penny Lane (song) 69
The People (newspaper) 123, 124
Philadelphia Inquirer (newspaper) 56
Phonetic reversal 41
Plastic Ono Band (performance group) 171
Playboy (magazine) 165
Podrazik, Walter 192
Polydor Records 88, 89
Polythene Pam (song) 22
Presley, Elvis 104, 125, 128, 151
Preston, Billy 9
The Providence (Rhode Island) Journal (newspaper) 193, 195

Q
Quantum Leap (TV program) 136
Queen Elizabeth 93
Question Mark and the Mysterians (performance group) 46

R
RCA Records 87
RKO Film and Television 44, 75, 81
Rain (song) 20, 41

Reeling In the Years (radio program) 136
Reinhart, Charles 192
Revolution 9 (song) 3, 4, 21, 41, 42, 57, 58, 66, 108, 166, 176
Revolver (LP) 105, 171
Reynolds, Frank 94
Reynolds, Jamie 27
Riders In the Sky (performance group) 131
Rider's Radio Theatre (radio program) 131
Rock and Other Four-Letter Words (book) 92
Rogalski, Pat 45
Rolling Stone (magazine) 60, 69, 104, 129, 151, 186, 188, 191
The Rolling Stones (performance group) 143
Roosevelt, Franklin 186
Rotary Connection (performance group) 27
Rowen and Martin's Laugh-In (TV program) 149, 187
Rubber Soul (LP) 105
Run For Your Life (song) 39, 157
Russ Gibb At Random (TV program) 129
Russ Gibb's Rock Chronicles (radio program) 129

S

Saint Paul (song) 142, 143, 144, 145, 146
San Francisco Chronicle (newspaper) 111, 112, 174
San Francisco Examiner (newspaper) 188
Sandherst, Rick 144
Saturday Night At the Cow Palace (song) 192
Saturday Night Live (TV program) 151
Savoy Truffle (song) 166
The Scaffold (performance group) 115, 116
Schacher, Mel 46
Schatzman, Leonard 187
Sellers, Peter 63
Sgt. Pepper's Lonely Hearts Club Band (LP) 9, 18, 19, 25, 27, 42, 43, 53, 57, 61, 76, 90, 103, 104, 116, 135, 153, 155, 156, 157, 158, 175
Sgt. Pepper's Reprise (song) 41, 157
Shakespere, William 31, 70, 163
She Said, She Said (song) 39, 81
Shea Stadium 47
Shears, Billy 71, 119, 156, 160, 197
Sheridan, Tony 88, 89
She's Leaving Home (song) 156
Silver Fox Records 85
Singleton, Shelby 85
Sixteen magazine 51
Sklar, Rick 59
"Sleepless In Seattle (film) 151
Small, John 47, 107, 108, 135
Smile (LP) 17, 18, 19, 21

Smiley Smile (LP) 19
Smith, Howard K. 93
Smith, Steve 193, 194, 195, 196
So Long, Paul (song) 13, 59, 87
Spector, Phil 65
St. Johns Wood 45, 92
Stairway to Heaven (song) 163
Star Trek (TV program) 36
Starr, Ringo 11, 18, 21, 22, 39, 52, 63, 65, 81, 145, 155, 156, 165, 194
Stevens, Wallace 183
Stone, George 99, 100, 101
Storybook Music (publishing company) 145
Strawberry Fields Forever (fanzine) 172, 198
Strawberry Fields Forever (song) 5, 19, 41, 107, 115, 149, 164
Sub Rosa Subway (song) 194
Suczek, Barbara 173
Sullivan, Jim 191
Sullivan, Peter 27
Summer, John 25, 27, 28, 29, 43, 44, 61, 100, 103, 120, 121, 122, 131, 197
Sun King (song) 22
Sutcliffe, Stuart 155
The Swinging Erudites (performance group) 149

T

Tate, Sharon 13
Tate-LaBianca murders

125
Taylor, Derek 14, 15, 45, 46, 51, 52, 65, 66, 92, 93, 174
Taylor, James 9
Tell Me What You See (song) 99
Terry Knight and the Pack (performance group) 46, 47, 141
Think For Yourself (radio program) 60
3 Saville Row 11
33 1/3 (LP) 194
Through the Looking Glass (book) 163
Time (magazine) 77, 112, 179
Tin Tin (performance group) 192
Tom 1, 3, 4, 5, 7, 13, 41, 75, 129, 145
Tome, Dino 196
Too Slim (aka, Fred LaBour) 131
Top Forty (radio trade publication) 60
Tosi, Dr. Oscar 68, 69
The Tragedy of King Lear (stageplay) 20, 31, 40, 70, 163
Truby, Dr. Henry M. 69
Tse-Tung, Mao 186
Tucker, Jack 27, 43, 44
Twain, Mark 65
Twiggy 142

U
UPI 29, 43, 44, 51, 59, 128
Ulvilden, Barb 28
University of Delaware 197
University of Miami 69, 174
University of Michigan

5, 7, 23, 33, 131, 147

V
Vance, James 127
Variety (magazine) 90, 106
Venus and Mars (LP) 194
Very Together (LP) 89
Vietnam War 7, 13, 33, 37, 124, 125
Volkswagen Beetle 35

W
WABC-AM (New York) 59, 100
WAKR-FM (Akron) 104
WCSX-FM (Detroit) 129
WDGY-TV (Minneapolis) 91
WDRC-FM (Providence, R.I.) 195
WEBN-FM (Cincinatti) 61
WFYC-AM (Alma, MI) 141
WGTB-FM (Washington, D.C.) 71
WIND-TV (Chicago) 91
WJBK-AM (Detroit) 141
WJR-AM (Detroit) 13
WKNR-FM (Detroit) 1, 5, 13, 14, 15, 17, 27, 39, 46, 47, 51, 60, 66, 68, 73, 76, 103, 107, 108, 113, 135, 145, 147, 163, 170, 174
WLS-TV (Chicago) 91
WMCA-AM (New York) 36, 63, 119, 174
WNEW-AM (New York) 60, 62, 99, 115
WOR-TV (New York) 79
WPLJ-AM (New York)

60
WSAI-AM (Cincinatti) 61, 62
WTAC-AM (Flint, MI) 141
WTIX-AM (New Orleans) 60, 85
WTOG-TV (Tampa/St. Petersburg) 131
WWDC-FM/AM (Washington, D.C.) 196
Walls and Bridges (LP) 194
Warhol, Andy 36
Warner Bros. Records 151
Washington Daily (newspaper) 126
Washington Evening Star (newspaper) 120, 156
Washington Post (newspaper) 92
Watergate 198
Wayne State University 69
We're All Paulbearers (song) 85
When I'm 64 (song) 19
While My Guitar Gently Weeps (song) 166
White Album (LP) 3, 11, 12, 33, 52, 90, 104, 107, 136, 164, 165, 166
Whitehead, Judge Jerry 127
Williams, Alan 198, 199
Wilson, Brian 19, 21, 106
Wings (performance group) 136
Within You, Without You (song) 157

Woloschuk, John 196
Woodstock 111
World Series 99

Y

Yager, Lewis 37, 56, 57,
   58, 100, 124, 134
Yellow Submarine (LP)
   120, 167
Yellow Submarine (song)
   21
Yesterday (song) 52,
   69, 103
Yesterday...and Today
   (LP) 105
Yonge, Roby 59
You Can't Do That
   (book) 192
You Never Give Me
   Your Money (song)
   22, 171
Your Mother Should
   Know (song) 48,
   113, 163

Z

Zacherias & The Tree
   People (perfor-
   mance group) 85